PUBLIC HEALTH IN THE 21ST CENTURY

NONPROFIT HOSPITALS AND THE COMMUNITY BENEFIT STANDARD

PUBLIC HEALTH IN THE 21ST CENTURY

Additional books in this series can be found on Nova's website under the Series tab.

Additional E-books in this series can be found on Nova's website under the E-books tab.

HEALTH CARE ISSUES, COSTS AND ACCESS

Additional books in this series can be found on Nova's website under the Series tab.

Additional E-books in this series can be found on Nova's website under the E-books tab.

PUBLIC HEALTH IN THE 21ST CENTURY

NONPROFIT HOSPITALS AND THE COMMUNITY BENEFIT STANDARD

MARIA G. REYES
EDITOR

Nova Science Publishers, Inc.
New York

For permission to use material from this book please contact us:
Telephone 631-231-7269; Fax 631-231-8175
Web Site: http://www.novapublishers.com

Additional color graphics may be available in the e-book version of this book.

LIBRARY OF CONGRESS CATALOGING-IN-PUBLICATION DATA

Nonprofit hospitals and the community benefit standard / editor, Maria G.
Reyes.
p. ; cm.
Includes bibliographical references and index.
ISBN 978-1-61761-999-1 (hardcover)
1. Voluntary hospitals--Government policy--United States. I. Reyes, Maria G.
[DNLM: 1. Hospitals, Voluntary--legislation & jurisprudence--United
States--Collected Works. 2. Community-Institutional Relations--legislation
& jurisprudence--United States--Collected Works. 3. Tax
Exemption--legislation & jurisprudence--United States--Collected Works. 4.
Tax Exemption--standards--United States--Collected Works. 5. Uncompensated
Care--legislation & jurisprudence--United States--Collected Works. WX 33
AA1]
RA971.3.N66 2010
362.11--dc22
2010041304

Published by Nova Science Publishers, Inc. † New York

CONTENTS

PREFACE

Non-profit hospitals receive billions of dollars in governmental subsidies due to their status as charitable organizations. Benefits that arise from this status under federal law include exemption from federal income taxes, eligibility to receive tax-deductible contributions, and authority to use tax-exempt bond financing. In recent years, Congress, the Internal Revenue Service (IRS), and members of the public have questioned whether hospitals are conducting sufficient charitable activities to justify these benefits. In the 111th Congress, the Patient Protection and Affordable Care Act, signed into law by President Obama on March 23, 2010, imposes additional requirements on these non-profit hospitals. This book examines the standard under which hospitals qualify for tax-exempt charitable status under federal law

Chapter 1- The recently enacted Patient Protection and Affordable Care Act (PPACA; P.L. 111-148, § 9007) imposes requirements on hospitals with § 501(c)(3) tax-exempt status. Under the act, hospitals will be required to regularly conduct "community health needs assessments" and adopt implementation strategies to meet those needs. They are also required to have written financial assistance and emergency medical care policies that are consistent with standards imposed by the act. Furthermore, hospitals are not able to charge eligible uninsured individuals more than the lowest amounts charged to insured individuals for emergency and other medically necessary care, and they must make reasonable efforts to determine an individual's eligibility for financial assistance before beginning extraordinary collection actions.

Chapter 2- Nonprofit hospitals qualify for federal tax exemption from the Internal Revenue Service (IRS) if they meet certain requirements. Since 1969, IRS has not specified that these hospitals have to provide charity care to meet these requirements, so long as they engage in activities that benefit the community. Many of these activities are intended to benefit the approximately 47 million uninsured individuals in the United States who need financial and other help to obtain medical care. Previous studies indicated that nonprofit hospitals may not be defining community benefit in a consistent and transparent manner that would enable policymakers to hold them accountable for providing benefits commensurate with their tax-exempt status. GAO was asked to examine (1) IRS's community benefit standard and the states' requirements, (2) guidelines nonprofit hospitals use to define the components of community benefit, and (3) guidelines nonprofit hospitals use to measure and report the components of community benefit. To address these objectives, GAO analyzed federal and state laws; the standards and guidance from federal agencies and industry groups; and 2006 data from California, Indiana, Massachusetts, and Texas. GAO also interviewed federal and state officials, and industry group representatives.

Chapter 3- The various tax exemptions provided to nonprofit hospitals have come under scrutiny by policymakers, with the central concern being whether those hospitals provide community benefits that justify forgone government tax revenues. In this paper, the Congressional Budget Office (CBO) measures the provision of certain community benefits and compares nonprofit hospitals with for-profit hospitals. For-profit hospitals do not receive tax exemptions and are not required to meet community-benefit standards; the level of community benefits provided by for-profit hospitals serves, therefore, as a useful benchmark against which to compare nonprofit hospitals. The analysis also examines the provision of community benefits by nonfederal government hospitals.[1]

Chapter 4- The federal government exempts nonprofit hospitals from federal income taxation and allows them to issue tax-exempt debt. To qualify for those tax advantages, the hospitals must provide community benefits, which the Internal Revenue Service (IRS) defines as promoting the health of any broad class of people, perhaps including such activities as charity care, health screening, community education about health risks, emergency room services, and basic research. In effect, nonprofit hospitals are thus required to provide services that may differ somewhat from those provided by for- profit hospitals. Analysts and policymakers have questioned, however, the degree to which the activities of nonprofit and for-profit hospitals actually differ and whether any resulting community benefits are sufficient to justify the tax benefits that nonprofits receive.

In: Nonprofit Hospitals and the Community... ISBN: 978-1-61761-999-1
Editor: Maria G. Reyes

Chapter 1

501(C)(3) HOSPITALS AND THE COMMUNITY BENEFIT STANDARD

Erika K. Lunder and Edward C. Liu

SUMMARY

The recently enacted Patient Protection and Affordable Care Act (PPACA; P.L. 111-148, § 9007) imposes requirements on hospitals with § 501(c)(3) tax-exempt status. Under the act, hospitals will be required to regularly conduct "community health needs assessments" and adopt implementation strategies to meet those needs. They are also required to have written financial assistance and emergency medical care policies that are consistent with standards imposed by the act. Furthermore, hospitals are not able to charge eligible uninsured individuals more than the lowest amounts charged to insured individuals for emergency and other medically necessary care, and they must make reasonable efforts to determine an individual's eligibility for financial assistance before beginning extraordinary collection actions.

The act's requirements appear to reflect concerns that have arisen in recent years about whether non-profit hospitals are providing adequate public benefits to justify their tax-exempt status. Nonprofit hospitals are eligible for federal tax-exempt status as charitable organizations described in § 501 (c)(3) of the Internal Revenue Code (IRC). Under the "community benefit" standard developed by the IRS, charitable hospitals are judged on whether they provide sufficient health benefits to the community. The IRS has recently developed a new annual reporting requirement (Schedule H of the Form 990) for hospitals to report information regarding their activities.

This chapter examines the standard under which hospitals qualify for tax-exempt charitable status under federal law, recent inquiries made by Congress and the IRS into whether hospitals are conducting sufficient activities to justify their exemption, and Section 9007 of the Patient Protection and Affordable Care Act. The **Appendix** to the report discusses the new Schedule H in detail.

Non-profit hospitals receive billions of dollars in governmental subsidies due to their status as charitable organizations.[1] Benefits that arise from this status under federal law include exemption from federal income taxes, eligibility to receive tax-deductible contributions, and authority to use tax-exempt bond financing.[2] In recent years, Congress, the Internal Revenue Service (IRS), and members of the public have questioned whether hospitals are conducting sufficient charitable activities to justify these benefits. In the 111th Congress, the Patient Protection and Affordable Care Act (PPACA), signed into law by President Obama on March 23, 2010 (P.L. 111-148), imposes additional requirements on § 501(c)(3) hospitals.[3]

STANDARD FOR § 501(C)(3) CHARITABLE STATUS

Non-profit hospitals typically qualify for federal tax-exempt status as charitable organizations described in § 501 (c)(3) of the Internal Revenue Code (IRC).[4] There is no definition in the tax code for the term "charitable." A regulation promulgated by the Treasury Department provides some guidance, although it does not explicitly address the activities of hospitals. It states that "[t]he term *charitable* is used in section 501(c)(3) in its generally accepted legal sense," and provides examples of charitable purposes, including the relief of the poor or unprivileged; the promotion of social welfare; and the advancement of education, religion, and science.[5]

In the absence of explicit statutory or regulatory requirements applying the term "charitable" to hospitals, it has been left to the IRS to determine the criteria hospitals must meet to qualify as § 501(c)(3) charitable organizations. Over the years, the IRS has developed two distinct standards: the "charity care standard" and the "community benefit standard."

Charity Care Standard

In 1956, the IRS issued Revenue Ruling 56-185, which addressed the requirements a hospital needed to meet in order to qualify for § 501(c)(3) status as a charitable organization.[6] One of these requirements is known as the "charity care standard." The standard required a hospital to provide, to the extent of its financial ability, free or reduced-cost care to patients unable to pay for it. A hospital that expected full payment did not, according to the ruling, provide charity care based on the fact that some patients ultimately failed to pay. The ruling noted that publicly supported community hospitals would normally qualify as charitable organizations because they serve the entire community, and a low level of charity care would not affect a hospital's exempt status if it was due to the surrounding community's lack of charitable demands.

Community Benefit Standard

In 1969, the IRS issued Revenue Ruling 69-545, which eliminated from Revenue Ruling 56-185 the requirement that a hospital provide free or reduced-cost care.[7] Under the standard developed in Revenue Ruling 69-545, which is known as the "community benefit standard," hospitals are judged on whether they promote the health of a broad class of individuals in the community.

The ruling involved a hospital that only admitted individuals who could pay for the services (by themselves, private insurance, or public programs such as Medicare), but operated a full-time emergency room that was open to everyone. The IRS ruled that the hospital qualified as a charitable organization because it promoted the health of people in its community. The IRS reasoned that because the promotion of health was a charitable purpose according to the general law of charity, it fell within the "generally accepted legal sense" of the term "charitable," as required by Treasury regulation.[8] Expanding on this point, the ruling stated that

> The promotion of health, like the relief of poverty and the advancement of education and religion, is one of the purposes in the general law of charity that is deemed beneficial to the community as a whole even though the class of beneficiaries eligible to receive a direct benefit from its activities does not include all members of the community, such as indigent members of the

> community, provided that the class is not so small that its relief is not of benefit to the community.[9]

The IRS concluded that the hospital was "promoting the health of a class of persons that is broad enough to benefit the community" because its emergency room was open to all and it provided care to everyone who could pay, whether directly or through third-party reimbursement.[10] Other characteristics of the hospital that the IRS highlighted included the following: its surplus funds were used to improve patient care, expand hospital facilities, and advance medical training, education, and research; it was controlled by a board of trustees that consisted of independent civic leaders; and hospital privileges were available to all qualified physicians.

It appears the community benefit standard was adopted partly in response to the enactment in 1965 of Medicare and Medicaid, which some thought would reduce the need for hospitals to provide charity care.[11] Its adoption by the IRS may also have been a response to concerns about the charity care standard. These concerns were evidenced in a legislative proposal, introduced in the same year Revenue Ruling 69-545 was issued, that would have created an explicit category in IRC § 501(c)(3) for hospitals.[12] The House Report accompanying the bill expressed concern with how the charity care standard was applied in practice:

> In a number of cases internal revenue agents have challenged the exempt status of hospitals on the sole ground that the hospitals are accepting insufficient numbers of patients at no charge or at rates substantially below cost. This has resulted in significant uncertainty as to the extent to which a hospital must accept patients who are unable to pay, in order to retain its exempt status.[13]

Shortly after the House Report was released, the IRS issued Revenue Ruling 69-545. The Senate Finance Committee then removed the hospital provision from the bill, noting the existence of the new ruling and stating it would look at the issue when it addressed pending Medicare and Medicaid legislation.[14] A subsequent Finance Committee staff document on Medicare and Medicaid issues advocated that the ruling be revoked and the charity care standard be reimposed until Congress could address the situation.[15]

Legal Challenge to the Community Benefit Standard

After the release of Revenue Ruling 69-545, several indigents and organizations with indigent members filed a class action suit challenging the IRS's authority to implement the community benefit standard, which they argued was inconsistent with the term "charitable" in IRC § 501 (c)(3) because it did not require treatment of the poor. The Supreme Court ordered the district court to dismiss the case because the plaintiffs lacked the constitutionally required standing to bring suit.[16] To have standing, "[a] plaintiff must allege personal injury fairly traceable to the defendant's allegedly unlawful conduct and likely to be redressed by the requested relief."[17] The plaintiffs' alleged injury was that the adoption of the community benefit standard had encouraged hospitals to not provide necessary medical care to the indigents. The Court, in holding the plaintiffs lacked standing, reasoned that it was "purely speculative" as to whether the hospitals had denied treatment because of the new ruling and not for other reasons and whether the plaintiffs' success would result in care being provided since hospitals could choose to give up their tax-exempt status if the cost was too high.[18]

Further Development of the Community Benefit Standard

The IRS continues to use and develop the community benefit standard. In 1983, the IRS issued Revenue Ruling 83-157, which clarifies the requirement that a hospital operate an emergency room that is open to the public.[19] While an important factor in Revenue Ruling 69-545 was that the hospital operated an emergency room open to everyone, Revenue Ruling 83-157 states that a hospital without an emergency room may still qualify for exempt status if other conditions are met. The ruling recognized there are circumstances in which hospitals may not need to operate emergency rooms, such as when a state agency has determined that its operation would be duplicative or when a hospital is in a specialized field that is unlikely to require emergency care. In these situations, a hospital may still qualify as a charitable organization if it shows other evidence that it provides benefits to the community by promoting the health of a broad class of persons. The ruling listed examples of factors that may be used as evidence: a board of directors chosen from members of the community; an open medical staff policy; treatment of patients using public programs (e.g., Medicare and Medicaid); and using surplus funds for improving patient care, facilities, equipment, and medical training, education, and research.

RECENT CONTROVERSY

In the past several years, questions have arisen as to whether non-profit hospitals deserve the benefits they receive as § 501(c)(3) charitable organizations.[20] Areas of controversy include the prices charged to low-income uninsured patients for medical care in comparison to those charged patients paying through insurance; the methods used by hospitals to collect payment from patients and the classification of bad debt as a community benefit; an increasing number of partnerships between tax-exempt hospitals and for-profit entities; and the amount of compensation paid to high-level employees. Additionally, some have questioned whether the community benefit standard is correct, or whether tax-exempt hospitals should categorically be required to provide a certain level of charity care.

In 2004 and 2005, class action lawsuits were filed in at least 25 states challenging the treatment and billing practices of § 501(c)(3) hospitals with respect to low-income uninsured individuals.[21] One claim made by the plaintiffs was that IRC § 501(c)(3) created a contract between the federal government and hospitals or a charitable trust for the public's benefit, either of which required hospitals to provide emergency treatment to patients regardless of their ability to pay, charge affordable and fair prices, and not engage in abusive collection practices. Courts disagreed, finding that the statute clearly neither creates a contract or charitable trust, nor provides third- party beneficiaries with a private cause of action.[22]

Congressional Activity in the 109th and 110th Congresses

Over the past several years, the activities of § 501 (c)(3) hospitals have received congressional attention. For example, in the 109th Congress, the House Ways and Means and Senate Finance Committees held hearings on tax-exempt hospitals.[23] Additionally, then-Chairman Thomas of the Ways and Means Committee introduced the Tax Exempt Hospitals Responsibility Act of 2006 (H.R. 6420, 109th Congress). Under the bill, a hospital would have only been eligible for § 501(c)(3) status if it (1) adopted policies and procedures, consistent with requirements imposed by the act, for providing and charging for medically necessary care to low-income uninsured individuals, and (2) normally operated in a manner consistent with those policies and procedures. No action was taken on the bill.

In the 110th Congress, the minority staff on the Senate Finance Committee released a discussion draft of possible tax-exempt hospital reforms and invited public comment on them.[24] Among the proposals put forth in the discussion draft were a requirement that each hospital maintain and publicize a charity care program and provide minimum amounts of charity care measured as a percentage of that hospital's total operating expenses. At the request of Senator Grassley, the Government Accountability Office (GAO) issued a report that examined how the discretion afforded hospitals under federal law in determining their community benefit activities and the wide variety in state community benefit requirements have led to inconsistencies in the way community benefits are defined and measured. [25]

Recent IRS Activity and Schedule H of Form 990

In 2006, the IRS sent questionnaires to approximately 600 large hospitals to collect information on how hospitals operated (e.g., billing practices, emergency room availability, and compensation) and what types of community benefits they provided. [26] Amid concerns about "whether there [were] differences between for-profit and tax-exempt hospitals,"[27] the IRS announced that hospitals would be required to provide additional information specific to their industry on a new Schedule H of the redesigned Form 990 (the annual information return filed by tax-exempt organizations).[28] Schedule H was drafted to "combat the lack of transparency surrounding the activities of tax-exempt organizations that provide hospital or medical care."[29]

Schedule H contains six parts, which are discussed in detail in the **Appendix**. Part I requests details about a hospital's charity care program and attempts to quantify charity care expenditures. Part II quantifies the hospital's community building activities. Part III quantifies the costs due to Medicare shortfalls and bad debts owed to the organization. Part IV requires disclosure of any joint ventures in which a hospital participates. Part V requests information about the entity's health care facilities. Part VI provides an area in which to discuss, in a narrative fashion, other charitable activities that may be difficult to quantify. For tax year 2008, the only portion of Schedule H that was required was the disclosure and description of the hospital facilities operated by the filing entity. The entire Schedule is mandatory beginning with tax year 2009.

PATIENT PROTECTION AND AFFORDABLE CARE ACT

The Patient Protection and Affordable Care Act (PPACA; P.L. 111-148, § 9007) imposes additional requirements on hospitals in order to qualify for § 501(c)(3) status. The requirements apply to organizations operating a facility that must be licensed, registered, or similarly recognized as a hospital under state law and any other organization determined by the Treasury Secretary to have the provision of hospital care as its principal § 501 (c)(3) tax-exempt function or purpose.[30] An organization with multiple facilities must meet the requirements for each facility and will not be treated as a § 501(c)(3) organization with respect to any facility for which the requirements are not met.

The act imposes four new requirements.[31] First, starting with taxable years beginning after March 23, 2012, hospitals will be required to conduct a "community health needs assessment" in the current or past two taxable years and adopt an implementation strategy to meet those needs.[32] The assessment must be made publicly available and take into account input from persons representing the broad interests of the community, including those with public health knowledge or expertise. An organization that fails to meet the assessment requirement for the taxable year will be subject to a new excise tax equal to $50,000.[33] Additionally, hospitals will be required to describe on the Form 990 how the needs identified in the assessment are being met and explain why any identified needs are not being addressed.[34]

Second, starting with taxable years beginning after March 23, 2010, hospitals are required to have written financial assistance and emergency medical care policies.[35] The financial assistance policy must address eligibility criteria for financial assistance, the application process, and whether the assistance includes free or discounted care. Other issues that must be addressed include the basis for calculating amounts charged to patients, the actions that might be taken for nonpayment (e.g., collection actions and reporting to credit agencies),[36] and the hospital's measures to widely publicize the policy within the community. The emergency medical care policy must require the hospital to provide, "without discrimination," care for emergency medical conditions[37] to individuals regardless of their eligibility for financial assistance.

Third, with respect to emergency and other medically necessary care, hospitals may not charge individuals eligible under the financial assistance policy more than the lowest amounts charged to those with insurance coverage.[38] Hospitals are also prohibited from using gross charges. These rules apply to taxable years beginning after March 23, 2010.

Fourth, hospitals are required to make reasonable efforts to determine whether an individual is eligible for financial assistance before beginning extraordinary collection actions.[39] This provision applies to taxable years beginning after March 23, 2010.

The Treasury Department is directed to issue necessary regulations and guidance, including guidance on whether a hospital has made reasonable efforts to determine a patient's eligibility under its financial assistance policy.[40] An official at the Treasury Department has been quoted as saying that guidance on the act's provisions is needed "sooner rather than later," although she did not offer specifics.[41]

Under the act, the Treasury Secretary will also be required to review, at least once every three years, the community benefit activities of any hospital subject to the new requirements.[42] Additionally, he or she, in consultation with the Secretary of Health and Human Services (HHS), will be required to annually provide Congress with information on the charity care, bad debt expenses, and unreimbursed costs for services provided under means and non-means tested government programs of private tax-exempt, taxable, and government-owned hospitals, in addition to the costs of community benefit activities by private tax-exempt hospitals.[43] A report on trends in this information is due within five years of the act's enactment.

APPENDIX. SCHEDULE H

As discussed in this chapter, hospitals with tax-exempt status are now required to provide information specific to their industry on the new Schedule H of the redesigned Form 990 (the annual information return filed by tax-exempt organizations).[44] The IRS released a draft Schedule H in June 2007 and, after seeking public comment on the draft, issued the final version in December 2007. Drawn heavily from, but not identical to, the community benefit reporting model used by the Catholic Health Association of the United States (CHA), Schedule H was drafted to "combat the lack of transparency surrounding the activities of tax-exempt organizations that provide hospital or medical care."[45]

Comments on the draft expressed immediate concerns about the technical and procedural implications of the addition. For example, comments reflected uncertainty over what constituted a hospital and whether multiple iterations of the Schedule were required for entities operating more than one hospital facility. In response, the IRS indicated that it intended to defer to state law for the definition of hospitals and that only one Schedule H would be required for an entity with a single employer identification number, regardless of the number of hospitals run by it.[46]

Schedule H contains six parts, each of which will be discussed in detail below. Part I requests details about a hospital's charity care program and attempts to quantify charity care expenditures. Part II quantifies the hospital's community building activities. Part III quantifies the costs due to Medicare shortfalls and bad debts owed to the organization. Part IV requires disclosure of any joint ventures in which a hospital participates. Part V requests information about the entity's health care facilities. Part VI provides an area in which to discuss, in a narrative fashion, other charitable activities that may be difficult to quantify.

Part I: Quantifying the "Community Benefit" Standard

Part I attempts to quantify the amount of community benefit provided by hospitals on an annual basis. The metric the IRS has chosen to quantify community benefit is dollars spent. Qualifying expenses include free care, unreimbursed Medicaid, unreimbursed costs from other means tested government programs,[47] community health improvement services,[48] health professions education,[49] subsidized health services,[50] research,[51] and contributions to other community groups.[52]

Aside from concerns about the technical aspects of the new Schedule H, several substantive criticisms also emerged from the public comments. For the most part, these criticisms stemmed from the perception that the categories of charity care and community benefit envisioned by the IRS were underinclusive.[53] The agency had explicitly stated in its comments accompanying the initial draft of Schedule H that the Schedule was an attempt to "quantify, in an objective manner, the community benefit standard applicable to tax-exempt hospitals."[54] While the IRS did not suggest a minimum level of expenditures that would be required in order to justify tax-exemption, it is probable that some hospitals were concerned that the exclusion of certain expenditures would make themselves appear, on paper, undeserving of tax-exempt status. By and large, these criticisms focused on three specific omissions: community building expenditures, Medicare shortfalls, and bad debt.

Part II: Community Building

Schedule H includes an area, Part II, in which to report community building expenditures. Although the definition of "community building" may not be obvious at first glance, it is generally understood to refer to programs that are intended to have a beneficial impact upon the health of a community but that do not provide medical care.[55] Examples of community building are housing improvements, economic development, community support, environmental improvements, leadership development, coalition building, community health improvement advocacy, and workforce development.[56]

The initial draft of Schedule H did not include community building activities in its calculation of community benefit. In comments on the draft, the CHA strongly opposed their exclusion. The CHA argued that "there is clear consensus in the public health community that social and environmental factors are strong determinants of health for vulnerable populations," citing publications from the Centers for Disease Control and Prevention and other scholarly articles.[57] Additionally, the CHA noted that "every community building activity would qualify for exemption on a stand-alone basis."[58]

Despite the subsequent inclusion of community building metrics on the Schedule H, these numbers are still separate from the reporting of charity care and community benefit expenditures in Part I. The IRS commentary on the Schedule's final draft reflected the view that the link between community building and health was still tenuous and that the reporting tools in Schedule H are intended to operate, in part, as data collection methods for the IRS to discern what links exist.[59]

Part III: Medicare Shortfalls

Hospitals incur costs when treating all patients, including patients who are covered by Medicare. Medicare, however, may not reimburse a provider for the total cost of services received by a patient. The difference between the Medicare reimbursement rates and the costs incurred by a hospital are called shortfalls.

Some commentators on the draft Schedule H expressed a belief that a hospital should be allowed to include the aggregate amount of these shortfalls in any calculation of the total community benefit provided by that hospital. For example, comments from the Health Law and Taxation Sections of the American Bar Association (ABA) reasoned that "the entire amount of any 'Medicare shortfall' should count as 'charity care,' because the elderly constitute a clearly recognized charitable class."[60] Additionally, the American Hospital Association (AHA) commented that "many Medicare beneficiaries, like their Medicaid counterparts, are poor," and would have qualified for a hospital's charity care program or Medicaid in addition to Medicare.[61] If these patients had been treated as charity care, the entire cost of medical care would have been considered community benefit under Part I. Additionally, any shortfall in Medicaid reimbursement would similarly have been included in community benefit.

Others, however, argued that Medicare shortfalls are not a useful metric for determining community benefit. The Catholic Health Association, opposing inclusion, noted that "many for- profit hospitals compete aggressively for these [Medicare] patients."[62] In its view, measuring Medicare shortfalls would not usefully distinguish for-profit hospitals from those seeking tax exemption, and creating distinctions between these two groups is necessary to ensure that tax exemption retains its credibility with policy makers. Notwithstanding these arguments, the CHA noted that "if, at some point, access problems emerge for Medicare patients, the rationale for including Medicare services as community benefit increases."[63]

Schedule H includes a dedicated area in which to report Medicare shortfalls. Despite the addition of Part III, the IRS does not treat Medicare shortfalls as a direct measure of community benefit, in and of themselves. Instead, hospitals are asked to "[d]escribe ... the extent to which any shortfall reported in [this part] *should* be considered as community benefit."[64]

Part III (continued): Bad Debt

Hospitals regularly engage in billing and collection practices in order to recoup co-pays, deductibles, and other expenses from patients. During the collection process, there may occur a point at which it becomes apparent that a debt owed to the hospital has little or no potential of repayment. In accordance with sound accounting practices, it is customary to "write off" these debts as "bad debt."

Because bad debts, by definition, represent services hospitals have provided without compensation, some believe that the aggregate amount of bad debt should be included in any calculation of community benefit. Community benefit in the context of the provision of health care services normally refers to means-tested eligibility programs, but the ABA noted that hospitals continue to have difficulty separating traditional uncompensated care from true bad debt" due to "issues associated with identifying individuals who qualify for uncompensated care."[65] Some portion of bad debt, therefore, appears to include the provision of care to individuals who would have been eligible for charity care.[66] Proponents argue that it is unfair to penalize a hospital with a reduced community benefit calculation simply because the charity care program did not accurately classify these individuals.[67]

Support for inclusion of bad debt was not universal among the comments submitted. The Catholic Health Association noted that bad debt is a "'cost of doing business' that affects taxable and tax- exempt organizations."[68] In CHA's opinion, reporting bad debt does not create meaningful distinctions between for-profit and non-profit entities that would justify tax exemption.[69] CHA did not necessarily dispute the theory that bad debt includes some patient charges that should be considered charity care. Rather, CHA argued that hospitals should improve their charity care programs to identify these patients at the onset of treatment, rather than using bad debt to approximate the impact of these patients after the fact.[70] In support of this argument, CHA also noted that "many Catholic hospitals have changed their policies and improved their ability to identify patients eligible for financial assistance."[71] Some patient advocates have also noted the perceived inequity in allowing hospitals to benefit from bad debt after instituting potentially aggressive and damaging collection practices against patients.[72]

Schedule H allows hospitals to report bad debt in Part III alongside Medicare shortfalls, but bad debt expense may not be reported on the charity care and community benefit table.[73] As with Medicare shortfalls, filing hospitals will have to explain what portion of bad debt should be considered community benefit.[74] The IRS comments accompanying the Schedule's final draft indicated that it does not intend to automatically consider any portion of bad debt a community benefit, citing a lack of consensus regarding bad debt policies among hospitals.[75]

Part IV: Management Companies and Joint Ventures

Part IV of Schedule H asks tax-exempt entities that operate hospitals to list the joint ventures they participate in. Joint ventures can be problematic in the non-profit healthcare context for a variety of reasons. If physicians with staff privileges at the hospital also have a proprietary interest in the joint venture, referrals to that joint venture may violate federal prohibitions against self-referrals or kickbacks.[76] If directors or trustees of the hospital have a proprietary interest in that joint venture, the non-profit status of the hospital could be jeopardized by any benefit that they receive as a result of their interest in the venture.[77] Similarly, in *St. David's Health Care System v. United States*, the Fifth Circuit held that a joint venture's profit motive could undermine a non-profit partner's status as a charitable organization.[78]

For the most part, these issues are common to all tax-exempt organizations. The majority of comments addressing this issue noted that the IRS already receives information on joint ventures in the redesigned Form 990, and that only organizations that operate hospitals are burdened with this extra reporting requirement in Schedule H.[79] In response, the IRS noted that the "unique relationship between hospitals and physicians resulting from their special status of having medical staff privileges without regard to employment appears to have no clear analogy in other exempt organization contexts."[80] The IRS did limit this reporting requirement to those joint ventures where directors, trustees, and physicians with staff privileges together owned at least 10% of the joint venture.

Part V: Facility Information

Organizations are asked, in Part V of Schedule H, to identify all hospital or medical care facilities and to indicate the types of medical services provided by each. The definition of hospital or medical care does *not* include assisted living services, vocational training for the disabled, or medical education and research.[81]

Part VI: Supplemental Information

Part VI of Schedule H provides an area in which to provide narrative information regarding the amount of community benefit provided. The IRS stated that this area could be used to explain why some portion of Medicare shortfall or bad debt reported in other areas of the Schedule should be considered community benefit.[82] In addition, hospitals may provide details about other community benefits they provide that are not easily quantifiable.[83]

End Notes

1 *See* Congressional Budget Office, NONPROFIT HOSPITALS AND THE PROVISION OF COMMUNITY BENEFITS, Dec. 2006, at 5 (reporting the estimated value of federal and state tax exemptions provided to charitable hospitals in 2002 was $12.6 billion).

2 *See* IRC §§ 501(a), 170(c)(2), 145.

3 The act's provisions are codified at IRC §§ 501(r), 4959, and 6033(b)(15).

4 IRC § 501(c)(3) describes entities "organized and operated exclusively for religious, charitable, scientific, testing for public safety, literary, or educational purposes, or to foster national or international amateur sports competition ... or for the prevention of cruelty to children or animals ...." Among other criteria, "no part of the [organization's] net earnings ... [may] inure[] to the benefit of any private shareholder or individual." Some hospitals may qualify to be § 501(c)(3) educational or scientific organizations. *See* Rev. Rul. 56-185; 1956-1 C.B. 202. Non-profit hospitals might also be able to qualify for exemption as § 501(c)(4) social welfare organizations.

5 Treas. Reg. § 1.501(c)(3)-1(d)(2).

6 Rev. Rul. 56-185, 1956-1 C.B. 202.

7 Rev. Rul. 69-545, 1969-2 C.B. 117.

8 *Id.* (citing to Restatement (Second), Trusts, §§ 368, 372; IV Scott on Trusts (3rd ed. 1967), §§ 368, 372).

9 *Id.* (citing to Restatement (Second), Trusts, § 368, comment (b); § 372, comments (b), (c); IV Scott on Trusts (3rd ed. 1967), §§ 368, 372).

10 *Id.*

11 *See* STAFF OF S. COMM. ON FINANCE, 91ST CONG., MEDICARE AND MEDICAID: PROBLEMS, ISSUES, AND ALTERNATIVES, at 56 (Comm. Print 1970) [hereinafter *Staff Report*].

12 Tax Reform Act of 1969, H.R. 13270, 91st Cong. (1969) (enacted into law, P.L. 91-172, without the hospital provision).

13 H.Rept. 91-413, pt. 1, at 43 (1969).

14 S.Rept. 9 1-552, at 61 (1969).

15 *See Staff Report*, *supra* note 11, at 56 ("The staff strongly recommends revocation of Revenue Ruling 69-545 in light of the recent legislative history and continuation of the prior position of the Service until such time as Congress can devise an alternative approach establishing reasonable yardsticks of charitable service related to the financial capacity of a hospital. Such action by the Service would assist in protecting the availability of necessary hospital care to Medicare, Medicaid, and other poor patients").

16 Simon v. E. Ky. Welfare Rights Org., 426 U.S. 26 (1976). The plaintiffs had prevailed before the district court, which had voided Revenue Ruling 69-545 as being "improperly promulgated" since there was insufficient justification for the "clear change of previously

administered policy." E. Ky. Welfare Rights Org. v. Shultz, 370 F. Supp. 325, 336- 38 (D.D.C. 1973). The D.C. Circuit Court of Appeals reversed, finding the IRS interpretation of "charitable" was permissible because the term's definition "has never been static and has been broadened in recent years" and "is thus capable of a definition far broader than merely the relief of the poor." E. Ky. Welfare Rights Org. v. Simon, 506 F.2d 1278, 1286-90 (D.C. Cir. 1974). The court reasoned that limiting the term to relief of the poor "fails to recognize the changing economic, social and technological precepts and values of contemporary society." *Id.* at. 1288.

[17] Allen v. Wright, 468 U.S. 737, 751 (1984).

[18] E. Ky. Welfare Rights Org., 426 U.S. at 42, 43.

[19] Rev. Rul. 83-157, 1983-2 C.B. 94.

[20] *See, e.g.,* John Carreyrou and Barbara Martinez, *Nonprofit Hospitals, Once For the Poor, Strike It Rich; With Tax Breaks, They Outperform For-Profit Rivals*, WALL ST. J., Apr 4, 2008, at A. 1.

[21] *See, e.g.,* McCoy v. E. Tex. Med. Ctr. Reg'l Healthcare Sys., 388 F. Supp. 2d 760 (E.D. Tex. 2005); Valencia v. Miss. Baptist Med. Ctr., Inc., 363 F. Supp. 2d 867 (S.D. Miss. 2005); Amato v. UPMC, 371 F. Supp. 2d 752 (W.D. Penn. 2004); Ferguson v. Centura Health Corp., 358 F. Supp. 2d 1014 (D. Colo. 2004); Quinn v. BJC Health Sys., 364 F. Supp. 2d 1046 (E.D. Mo. 2005). The Judicial Panel for Multidistrict Litigation denied a motion to consolidate the cases. *See In re* Not-for-Profit Hospitals/Uninsured Patients Litigation, 341 F. Supp. 2d 1354 (J.P.M.L. Oct. 19, 2004).

[22] *See, e.g.,* Kolari v. New York-Presbyterian Hosp., 382 F. Supp. 2d 562, 565-56 (S.D.N.Y. Mar. 29, 2005), *vacated, in part, and remanded*, 455 F.3d 118 (2d Cir. 2006) ("Plaintiffs here have lost their way; they need to consult a map or a compass or a Constitution because Plaintiffs have come to the judicial branch for relief that may only be granted by the legislative branch.").

[23] *Hearing on the Tax-Exempt Hospital Sector before the House Committee on Ways and Means*, 109th Cong. (2005),http://waysandmeans. house.gov/ hearings. asp? formmod e =detail& hearing=415; *Taking the Pulse of Charitable Care and Community Benefits at Nonprofit Hospitals: Hearing before the Senate Committee on Finance*, 109th Cong. (2006), available at http://finance.senate.gov/sitepages/hearing 091306.htm.

[24] Senate Finance Committee Minority Staff, *Tax-Exempt Hospitals: Discussion Draft* (2007), available at http://finance.senate.gov/press/Gpress/2007/prg071907a.pdf.

[25] U.S. Government Accountability Office, *Nonprofit Hospitals: Variation in Standards and Guidance Limits Comparison of How Hospitals Meet Community Benefit Requirements*, GAO-08-880, Sept. 2008. Some states have adopted charity care or community benefit requirements as a condition imposed to receive state tax exemption or for regulatory purposes. *See id., see also* Community Catalyst, Inc., *Health Care Community Benefits: A Compendium of State Laws*, available at http://www.communitycatalyst.org/doc_store/ publications/ community_benefits_compendium_2007.pdf.

[26] The questionnaire is available on the IRS website at http://www.irs.gov/pub/irs-tege/exhibit_1__form13790.pdf. The IRS's final report on the compliance project is available at http://www.irs.gov/pub/irs-tege/frepthospproj.pdf.

[27] IRS, *Draft Form 990 Redesign Project - Schedule H: Instructions*, at 1, June 14, 2007, at http://www.irs.gov/pub/irs-tege/draftform990redesign_schh_instr.pdf [hereinafter *June 14 Draft Comments*].

[28] IRS, Press Release, *IRS Releases Final 2008 Form 990 for Tax-Exempt Organizations, Adjusts Filing Threshold to Provide Transition Relief,* Dec. 20, 2007, available at http://www.irs.gov/newsroom/article/0,,id=176722,00 .html. The new Schedule H is part of a significant redesign of the entire Form 990.

[29] *June 14 Draft Comments, supra* note 27, at 1.

[30] IRC § 501(r)(2).

[31] IRC § 501(r)(1).

[32] IRC § 501(r)(3).
[33] IRC § 4959.
[34] IRC § 6033(b)(15). Hospitals will also be required to provide audited financial statements with the Form 990 and disclose amounts paid under the new excise tax.
[35] IRC § 501(r)(4).
[36] This information is only required if the hospital does not have a separate billing and collections policy.
[37] Emergency medical conditions are defined with reference to § 1867 of the Social Security Act (42 U.S.C. § 1395dd) also known as the Emergency Medical Treatment and Active Labor Act (EMTALA). EMTALA currently defines emergency medical conditions as any situation in which the absence of immediate medical care would jeopardize the patients health or lead to serious bodily impairment or dysfunction. This definition also explicitly includes women in labor where there is insufficient time to safely transfer the mother to another facility. 42 U.S.C. § 1395dd(e)(1). Under EMTALA, all Medicare participating hospitals that operate an emergency room, whether tax-exempt or not, are required to screen all incoming patients and stabilize emergency medical conditions regardless of ability to pay. For more information, *see* CRS Report RS22738, *EMTALA: Access to Emergency Medical Care*, by Edward C. Liu.
[38] IRC § 501(r)(5).
[39] IRC § 501(r)(6).
[40] IRC § 501(r)(7).
[41] Simon Brown, *Guidance Needed on New Charitable Hospital Provisions, Treasury Official Says*, TAX NOTES (May 3, 2010).
[42] PPACA, § 9007(c).
[43] PPACA, § 9007(e). The reports will go to the House Committees on Ways and Means, Education and Labor, and Energy and Commerce, and the Senate Committees on Finance and Health, Education, Labor, and Pensions.
[44]Schedule H is available at http://www.irs.gov/pub/irs-pdf/f990sh.pdf (hereinafter *Schedule H*).
[45] *June 14 Draft Comments, supra* note 27, at 1.
[46] IRS, *Form 990 Redesign for Tax Year 2008 Schedule H, Hospitals—Highlights*, at 2, Dec. 20, 2007, available at http://www.irs.gov/pub/irs-tege/highlights_schedule_h.pdf [hereinafter *Dec. 20 Draft Highlights*]. *See also* IRS, *Schedule H (Form 990) Instructions*, at 1, available http://www.irs.gov/pub/irs-pdf/i990sh.pdf [hereinafter *Schedule H Instructions*].
[47] Other means tested programs includes SCHIP and other federal, state, or local health care programs where "eligibility depends on the recipient's income or asset level." *Schedule H Instructions*, *supra* note 46, at 9.
[48] Community health improvement services must be supported by a documented "community need." *Id.* at 10.
[49] Costs for medical residents and interns may be included as health professions education costs. *Id.* at 11.
[50] Subsidized health services must be supported by a documented "community need." *Id.* at 13.
[51] Research funded by tax-exempt or government sources, including internally funded research, may be reported here. Research funded by other entities may not be reported as community benefit, but can be listed under Part VI of Schedule H. *Id.* at 14.
[52] *Schedule H, supra* note 44, at Part I.
[53] *See, e.g.*, American Hospital Association, *Comments on Draft Schedule H*, at 2-4, Aug. 21, 2007 [hereinafter AHA Comments]; Catholic Health Association of the United States, *Comments Related to Schedule H*, at 4, Sept. 12, 2007, [hereinafter CHA Comments]; Health Law and Taxation Sections of the American Bar Association, *Comments Concerning Discussion Draft of Redesigned Form 990 for Tax-exempt Organizations*, at 66-69, Oct. 4, 2007 [hereinafter ABA Comments].
[54] *June 14 Draft Comments, supra* note 27, at 1.

[55] *See, e.g.*, AHA Comments, *supra* note 53, at 7; CHA Comments, *supra* note 53, at 8; ABA Comments, *supra* note 53, at 69.
[56] *Schedule H, supra* note 44, at Part II.
[57] CHA comments, *supra* note 53, at 9.
[58] *Id.* at 10.
[59] *Dec. 20 Draft Highlights*, *supra* note 46, at 4.
[60] ABA Comments, *supra* note 53, at 66 (citing Rev. Rul. 1972-124, 1972-1 C.B. 145).
[61] AHA Comments, *supra* note 53, at 5.
[62] CHA Comments, *supra* note 53, at 14. The discussion of Medicare shortfalls may also raise the question whether shortfalls in reimbursement from *for-profit* insurers should also be counted as uncompensated care.
[63] *Id.*
[64] *Schedule H, supra* note 44, at Part III (emphasis added).
[65] ABA Comments, *supra* note 53, at 66.
[66] Uninsured or under-insured patients that cannot afford to pay are nevertheless charged, and that inevitably leads to bad debt precisely because they cannot afford to pay.
[67] One alternative put forth by the ABA is to include some percentage of bad debt, in proportion to the amount of bad debt universally in a given region, as community benefit. ABA Comments, *supra* note 53, at 67.
[68] CHA comments, *supra* note 53, at 15.
[69] *Id.*
[70] *Id.* at 14-15.
[71] *Id.* at 15.
[72] *See, e.g.*, Lucette Lagnado, *Twenty Years and Still Paying: Jeanette White is Long Dead But Her Hospital Bill Lives On*, WALL ST. J., Mar. 13, 2003, at B1.
[73] *Schedule H, supra* note 44, at Part III; *Schedule H Instructions*, *supra* note 44, at 3.
[74] *Schedule H, supra* note 44, at Part III.
[75] *Dec. 20 Draft Highlights*, *supra* note 46, at 3.
[76] For a more detailed discussion of physician self-referral and federal law, *see* CRS Report RL32494, *Medicare: Physician Self-Referral ("Stark I and II")*, by Jennifer O'Sullivan.
[77] Under IRC § 501(c)(3), the net earnings of a charitable organization may not flow to the benefit of any private shareholder or individual.
[78] St. David's Health Care System v. United States, 349 F.3d 232, 237 (5th Cir. 2003).
[79] *See, e.g.*, AHA Comments, *supra* note 53, at 8-9; CHA Comments, *supra* note 53, at 12-13; ABA Comments, *supra* note 53, at 73.
[80] *Dec. 20 Draft Highlights*, *supra* note 46 at 5.
[81] *June 14 Draft Comments*, *supra* note 27, at 8.
[82] *Dec. 20 Draft Highlights*, *supra* note 46, at 5.
[83] *Id.*; *see also* Schedule H, *supra* note 44, at Part VI.

In: Nonprofit Hospitals and the Community... ISBN: 978-1-61761-999-1
Editor: Maria G. Reyes

Chapter 2

NONPROFIT HOSPITALS: VARIATION IN STANDARDS AND GUIDANCE LIMITS COMPARISON OF HOW HOSPITALS MEET COMMUNITY BENEFIT REQUIREMENTS

United States Government Accountability Office

WHY GAO DID THIS STUDY

Nonprofit hospitals qualify for federal tax exemption from the Internal Revenue Service (IRS) if they meet certain requirements. Since 1969, IRS has not specified that these hospitals have to provide charity care to meet these requirements, so long as they engage in activities that benefit the community. Many of these activities are intended to benefit the approximately 47 million uninsured individuals in the United States who need financial and other help to obtain medical care. Previous studies indicated that nonprofit hospitals may not be defining community benefit in a consistent and transparent manner that would enable policymakers to hold them accountable for providing benefits commensurate with their tax-exempt status. GAO was asked to examine (1) IRS's community benefit standard and the states' requirements, (2) guidelines nonprofit hospitals use to define the components of community benefit, and (3) guidelines nonprofit hospitals use to measure and report the components of community benefit. To address these objectives, GAO analyzed federal and state laws; the standards and guidance from federal agencies and industry groups; and 2006 data from California, Indiana, Massachusetts, and Texas. GAO also interviewed federal and state officials, and industry group representatives.

IRS stated that the report in general was accurate, but noted several concerns regarding the description of the community benefit standard. CMS did not have any comments.

What GAO Found

IRS's community benefit standard allows nonprofit hospitals broad latitude to determine the services and activities that constitute community benefit. Furthermore, state community benefit requirements that hospitals must meet in order to qualify for state tax-exempt or nonprofit status vary substantially in scope and detail. For example, 15 states have community benefit requirements in statutes or regulations, and 10 of these states have detailed requirements.

GAO found that among the standards and guidance used by nonprofit hospitals, consensus exists to define charity care, the unreimbursed cost of means-tested government health care programs (programs for which eligibility is based on financial need, such as Medicaid), and many other activities that benefit the community as community benefit. However, consensus does not exist to define bad debt (the amount that the patient is expected to, but does not, pay) and the unreimbursed cost of Medicare (the difference between a hospital's costs and its payment from Medicare) as community benefit. Variations in the activities nonprofit hospitals define as community benefit lead to substantial differences in the amount of community benefits they report.

Even if nonprofit hospitals define the same activities as community benefit, they may measure the costs of these activities differently, which can lead to inconsistencies in reported community benefits. For example, standards and guidance vary on the level at which hospitals may report their community benefit (e.g., at an individual hospital level or a health care system level) and the method hospitals may use to estimate costs of community benefit activities. State data demonstrate that differences in how nonprofit hospitals measure charity care costs and the unreimbursed costs of government health care programs can affect the amount of community benefit they report.

With the added attention to community benefit has come a growing realization of the extent of variability among stakeholders in what should count and how to measure it. At present, determination and measurement of activities as community benefit for federal purposes are still largely a matter of individual hospital discretion. Given the large number of uninsured individuals, and the critical role of hospitals in caring for them, it is important that federal and state policymakers and industry groups continue their discussion addressing the variability in defining and measuring community benefit activities.

ABBREVIATIONS

AHA	American Hospital Association
BBRA	Medicare, Medicaid, and SCHIP Balanced Budget Refinement Act of 1999
CBO	Congressional Budget Office
CCR	cost-to-charge ratio
CHA	Catholic Health Association of the United States
CMS	Centers for Medicare & Medicaid Services
DSH	disproportionate share hospital
EIN	employer identification number
HFMA	Healthcare Financial Management Association
IRS	Internal Revenue Service
JCT	Joint Committee on Taxation
MedPAC	Medicare Payment Advisory Commission

September 12, 2008

The Honorable Charles E. Grassley
Ranking Member
Committee on Finance
United States Senate

Dear Senator Grassley:

In 2006, there were about 2,900 nonprofit hospitals in the United States.[1] These hospitals qualify for federal tax exemption from the Internal Revenue Service (IRS) if they meet certain requirements.[2] The exemption is based on the principle that the government's loss of tax revenues is offset by its relief from financial burdens that it would otherwise have to meet with appropriations from public funds, and by the benefits resulting from the promotion of general welfare.[3] In addition to federal income tax exemption, these hospitals also have access to charitable donations that are tax deductible to the donor and tax-exempt bond financing. Nonprofit hospitals may also be exempt under state law from state and local income, property, and sales taxes. The Joint Committee on Taxation (JCT)—a nonpartisan committee that assists Congress with tax legislation— estimated that in 2002, nonprofit hospitals received tax benefits of $12.6 billion at the federal, state, and local levels.[4]

To qualify for tax-exempt status, IRS requires nonprofit hospitals to be organized and operated exclusively for a charitable purpose. Before 1969, IRS specified that hospitals must provide charity care to meet this requirement.[5] Since 1969, however, IRS has not specified that nonprofit hospitals have to provide charity care to meet this requirement, but they must provide a benefit to the community. This has become known as the community benefit standard and has remained substantially unchanged since 1969. In addition to charity care, services and activities that can qualify as community benefits include the provision of health education and screening to specific vulnerable populations within the community and activities that benefit the greater public good, such as education for health professionals and medical research.

Many of these community benefit activities—especially charity care—are intended to benefit individuals who need financial and other help to obtain medical care. In 2006, there were approximately 47 million uninsured individuals in the United States.[6] These individuals are more likely than insured individuals to rely on hospital emergency rooms for medical care.[7] Some of these individuals with serious illness or injuries are admitted as inpatients to the hospital, incurring substantial treatment costs.[8] Because uninsured individuals may lack the ability to pay for their medical care, hospitals absorb some of the costs associated with providing uncompensated care—either through a charity care program or as expenses written off as bad debt.[9,10] Given the benefits available to tax- exempt hospitals, policymakers have been interested in determining the extent to which hospitals share the burden of caring for uninsured individuals.

In 2005, we reported on the amount of uncompensated care that nonprofit, for-profit, and government hospitals provided.[11] We found that nonprofit hospitals devoted only slightly more of their patient operating expenses to uncompensated care, on average, than their for-profit counterparts. We also found that the burden of uncompensated care was not evenly distributed among nonprofit hospitals—a small number of nonprofit hospitals provided substantially more uncompensated care than other hospitals receiving the same tax preference. In 2006, the Congressional Budget Office (CBO) also reported wide variation in the provision of uncompensated care among nonprofit hospitals.[12] These studies indicated that nonprofit hospitals may not be defining community benefit in a consistent manner that would enable policymakers to hold them accountable for providing benefits commensurate with their tax-exempt status.

Congress has since continued to raise questions about whether nonprofit hospitals sufficiently accept and share the burden of uncompensated care. As part of this effort, in 2007, you distributed a paper discussing potential reforms to the community benefit standard.[13] Among other things, you sought feedback on whether hospitals should be required to devote a minimum percentage of patient operating expenses or revenues (whichever is greater) to charity care in order to continue to qualify for federal tax exemption. You also expressed interest in gaining a better understanding of nonprofit hospitals' provision of community benefits in relation to their tax-exempt status, and raised concerns about the extent to which nonprofit hospitals define, measure, and report community benefits in a consistent and transparent manner.

To obtain more information on these topics, you asked us to describe IRS's community benefit standard and the states' community benefit requirements, and to examine guidelines nonprofit hospitals use to define, measure, and report the components of community benefit. In this chapter, we (1) determine the community benefit standard and requirements that IRS and the states have established; (2) examine the standards and guidance nonprofit hospitals use to define community benefit activities and their effects on reported community benefits; and (3) examine the standards and guidance nonprofit hospitals use to measure the costs of community benefit activities and their effects on reported community benefits.

To determine the community benefit standard that IRS has established, we examined relevant provisions of the Internal Revenue Code, IRS regulations, revenue rulings, and federal case law. To review states' community benefit requirements, we examined codified statutes and regulations of the states.[14]

To examine what activities are defined as community benefit, we reviewed standards and guidance from the following government agencies and industry groups: the Centers for Medicare & Medicaid Services (CMS), IRS, the American Hospital Association (AHA), the Catholic Health Association of the United States (CHA), VHA Inc.,[15] and the Healthcare Financial Management Association (HFMA). CMS, the agency that administers

Medicare,[16] requires cost information—including charity care costs and bad debt expenses—from hospitals that participate in Medicare.[17] AHA officials stated that it represents over three-fourths of the hospitals in the nation, including nonprofit hospitals. CHA represents Catholic health care organizations, including hospitals, and is the nation's largest group of nonprofit health care sponsors, systems, and facilities. VHA represents about 28 percent of the nation's community-owned, nonprofit hospitals. In 2006, CHA and VHA jointly released a set of detailed community benefit guidelines—*A Guide for Planning and Reporting Community Benefit.*[18] HFMA represents health care financial management executives and leaders in all areas of health care, including hospitals. In 2006, the organization issued financial reporting guidance on community benefit activities, including details on charity care and bad debt. In addition to examining standards and guidance from these organizations, we interviewed their officials and representatives. We also interviewed representatives from the Association of American Medical Colleges, which represents medical schools, teaching hospitals, and their faculty, residents, and students, as well as academic and professional societies; the Federation of American Hospitals, which represents for- profit community hospitals and health systems; the National Association of Children's Hospitals; state hospital associations and state health officials from California, Indiana, Massachusetts, and Texas; and seven nonprofit health care systems.[19]

To examine the effects of including or excluding various community benefit activities on reported community benefit, we analyzed 2006 state data from California, Indiana, Massachusetts, and Texas. We selected these four states because they represent diverse areas both geographically and in the percentage of hospitals that are nonprofit, and because they collected data on nonprofit hospitals' community benefits, which not many states maintain.[20] The state data were also the most recent available at the time of our analysis. We limited our analysis to nonprofit, nongovernmental, acute care, general hospitals that reported gross patient revenues and total operating expenses. We calculated and compared a variety of hospital expenses, including charity care costs, bad debt, unreimbursed costs of government health care programs,[21] and the costs of other activities that benefit the community, as percentages of total operating expenses. To assess the reliability of the state data from California, Indiana, Massachusetts, and Texas, we reviewed relevant documentation for each of the data sets and interviewed knowledgeable state officials about the accuracy of the data. Based on this information we determined that the state-collected data were reliable for the purposes of this chapter.

To examine practices nonprofit hospitals use to measure community benefit activities, we reviewed the standards and guidance from CMS, IRS, AHA, CHA and VHA, and HFMA. To examine the effects of these practices on reported community benefit, we analyzed 2006 state data from California, Indiana, Massachusetts, and Texas. Specifically, we compared the different ways hospitals calculate expenses, including charity care costs and the unreimbursed cost of Medicaid,[22] as percentages of total operating expenses. Appendix I contains a more complete description of our methodology. We conducted our work from July 2007 through August 2008 in accordance with generally accepted government auditing standards.

RESULTS IN BRIEF

IRS's community benefit standard allows nonprofit hospitals broad latitude to determine the services and activities that constitute community benefit. Furthermore, state community benefit requirements that hospitals must meet in order to qualify for state tax-exempt or nonprofit status vary substantially in scope and detail. For example, 15 states have community benefit requirements in statutes or regulations, and 10 of these states have detailed requirements.

Among the standards and guidance used by nonprofit hospitals, consensus exists to define charity care, the unreimbursed cost of means-tested government health care programs (programs for which eligibility is based on financial need, such as Medicaid), and many other activities that benefit the community as community benefit. However, consensus does not exist to define bad debt and the unreimbursed cost of Medicare as community benefit. Variations in the activities nonprofit hospitals define as community benefit lead to substantial differences in the amount of community benefits they report.

Even if nonprofit hospitals define the same activities as community benefit, they may measure the costs of those activities differently, which can lead to inconsistencies in reported community benefits. For example, standards and guidance vary on the level at which hospitals may report their community benefit (e.g., at an individual hospital level or a health care system level); the method hospitals may use to estimate costs of all community benefit activities; and the methods hospitals may use to measure costs of charity care, government health care programs, and other activities that benefit the community. State data demonstrate that differences in how nonprofit hospitals measure charity care costs and the unreimbursed costs of government health care programs can affect the amount of community benefit they report.

With the added attention to community benefit has come a growing realization of the extent of variability among stakeholders in what should count and how to measure it. At present, determination and measurement of activities as community benefit for federal purposes are still largely a matter of individual hospital discretion. Given the large number of uninsured individuals, and the critical role of hospitals in caring for them, it is important that federal and state policymakers and industry groups continue their discussion addressing the variability in defining and measuring community benefit activities. An encouraging prospect for the future is the potential availability of two national data sources derived from mandatory reporting to IRS and CMS. National data should be helpful in standardizing reporting on community benefit activities and informing public policy on the community benefit standard. However, the data from these two sources will not be available for analysis for several years, and it remains to be seen whether the data will be consistent and reliable.

CMS and IRS reviewed a draft of this chapter. CMS stated that it did not have any comments. IRS stated that the report in general was accurate, although the agency noted several concerns regarding the description of the community benefit standard. We addressed IRS's concerns as appropriate.

BACKGROUND

In 2006, the majority—59 percent—of the roughly 4,900 nonfederal, acute care general hospitals in the United States were nonprofit. The rest included government hospitals (25 percent) and for-profit hospitals (17 percent).[23] States varied—generally by region of the country—in their percentages of nonprofit hospitals (see Figure 1). States in the Northeast and Midwest had relatively high concentrations of nonprofit hospitals, whereas the concentration was relatively low in the South. For example, 88 percent of Massachusetts' hospitals were nonprofit, whereas only 32 percent of Texas' hospitals were nonprofit.

Sources: GAO analysis of 2006 CMS data; Map Resources (map).
Note: Hospitals include nonfederal, acute care, general hospitals.

Figure 1. Geographic Distribution of Nonprofit Hospitals in 2006

Among nonprofit hospitals we examined in California, Indiana, Massachusetts, and Texas, the average size of these hospitals, as measured by total operating expenses, varied (see table 1). For example, the average total operating expenses of nonprofit hospitals in Massachusetts were 98 percent higher than average total operating expenses of nonprofit hospitals in Indiana.

Table 1. Number of Nonprofit Hospitals and Their Average Total Operating Expenses in Selected States, 2006

	Number of hospitals	Average total operating expenses (in millions)
California	166	$201.3
Indiana	78	141.3
Massachusetts	64	279.6
Texas	119	148.9

Source: GAO analysis of 2006 California, Indiana, Massachusetts, and Texas data.
Note: Nonprofit hospitals include nongovernmental, acute care, general hospitals.

Federal Tax-Exemption Criteria for Nonprofit Hospitals

Federal tax exemption for charitable organizations has been in existence since the beginning of federal income tax law. This exemption is based on the principle that the government's loss of tax revenue is offset by its relief from financial burdens that it would otherwise have to meet with appropriations from public funds, and by the benefits resulting from the promotion of general welfare. Nonprofit hospitals have never been expressly categorized as tax-exempt organizations under section 501(c)(3) of the Internal Revenue Code. However, these hospitals are able to qualify for federal tax exemption under section 501(c)(3) of the Internal Revenue Code since IRS and courts have recognized the promotion of health for the benefit of the community—where medical assistance is afforded to the poor or where medical research is promoted—as a charitable purpose.[24] Specifically, nonprofit hospitals must be organized and operated exclusively for the promotion of health, ensuring that no part of their net earnings inure to the benefit of any private individual, and may not participate in political campaigns on behalf of any candidate or conduct substantial lobbying activities.[25]

IRS has also issued revenue rulings specifying how nonprofit hospitals can meet the requirements of federal tax exemption.[26] In a 1956 revenue ruling, IRS required tax-exempt hospitals to provide charity care to the extent of their financial abilities, which was known as the financial ability standard.[27] However, through another revenue ruling in 1969, IRS established the community benefit standard, which modified the charity care-based financial ability standard as to how hospitals could qualify for tax-exempt status.[28] The community benefit standard specified that nonprofit hospitals were not required to provide charity care to qualify for federal tax exemption, but they must provide a benefit to the community.[29] Therefore, nonprofit hospitals could qualify for tax-exempt status so long as they benefited the community in a way that relieved a governmental burden and promoted general welfare, even if not every member of the community received a direct benefit.

In the 1969 revenue ruling that established the community benefit standard, IRS recognized five factors that would support a nonprofit hospital's tax-exempt status. These five factors were (1) the operation of an emergency room open to all members of the community without regard to ability to pay;[30] (2) a governance board composed of community members; (3) the use of surplus revenue for facilities improvement, patient care, and medical training, education, and research; (4) the provision of inpatient hospital care for all persons in the community able to pay, including those covered by Medicare and Medicaid; and (5) an open medical staff[31] with privileges available to all qualifying physicians. IRS further stated that tax-exempt status would be determined based on the facts and circumstances of each case, and that neither the absence of particular factors set forth in the 1969 revenue ruling nor the presence of other factors would be necessarily conclusive.

Nonprofit hospitals that qualify for tax-exempt status are exempt from federal income taxation, have access to bond financing that generates tax-free interest earnings for the bondholder—allowing these hospitals to borrow funds at a lower cost than nonexempt entities—and are eligible to receive contributions that are tax deductible for the donors. In addition, these hospitals may also be exempt under state law from state and local income, property, and sales taxes, which in some cases are of a greater value than the federal income tax exemption.

Reporting of Community Benefit Information

Once nonprofit hospitals have applied for and are granted tax-exempt status by IRS, they must file Form 990 with IRS on an annual basis.[32] Form 990 collects information such as revenues and expenses, and program service accomplishments. In December 2007, IRS released a revised Form 990 to include a schedule specific to hospitals—Schedule H—that requires nonprofit hospitals to report their provision of activities that benefit the community in specified categories: charity care, bad debt, unreimbursed cost of government health care programs, and other activities that benefit the community.[33] The new hospital schedule will be mandatory starting in filing year 2010 for tax year 2009, and IRS officials have stated that complete data from the schedule may not be available until 2011, at the earliest.[34]

In addition to meeting IRS's community benefit reporting requirements, hospitals that participate in the Medicare program—including nonprofit hospitals—must file hospital cost reports with CMS.[35] The required cost report includes Worksheet S-10, which collects revenue and cost information on Medicaid, state and local indigent care programs, the State Children's Health Insurance Program,[36] and other uncompensated care— defined by CMS as charity care and bad debt—provided by the hospitals. CMS, in consultation with the Medicare Payment Advisory Commission (MedPAC),[37] is revising Worksheet S-10 as part of broader efforts to update the Medicare hospital cost report.

Beyond these two federal requirements, some states also require hospitals to report their provision of community benefits using state-specific reporting instruments. In addition, when requested, some hospitals also report their community benefits to the state hospital associations or other trade organizations to which they belong.

IRS's Standard Provides Broad Latitude for Nonprofit Hospitals to Determine Community Benefit Activities; State Requirements Vary Substantially in Scope and Detail

IRS's community benefit standard to qualify for tax-exempt status allows nonprofit hospitals broad latitude to determine the services and activities that constitute community benefit. Furthermore, state community benefit requirements that hospitals must meet in order to qualify for state tax- exempt or nonprofit status vary substantially in scope and detail.

IRS's Community Benefit Standard Provides Broad Latitude to Nonprofit Hospitals

IRS's community benefit standard that hospitals must meet to qualify for federal tax exemption provides broad latitude to the hospitals in determining the nature and amount of the community benefits they provide.[38] Specifically, IRS, in a 1969 revenue ruling that established the current community benefit standard, modified the existing tax-exemption requirement that focused primarily on the level of charity care that a hospital provided. This 1969 revenue ruling also listed the five factors that demonstrated how a nonprofit hospital could benefit the community in a way that relieved governmental burden and promoted general welfare.[39] While IRS recognized these five factors as supportive of a nonprofit hospital's tax-exempt status, it also stated that a nonprofit hospital seeking exemption need not meet all five factors to qualify for tax-exempt status; instead, the determination is based on all the facts and circumstances, and the absence of a particular factor may not necessarily be conclusive. As stated by the Commissioner of Internal Revenue, some of the five factors are now common practice in the hospital community and are less relevant in distinguishing tax-exempt hospitals from their for-profit counterparts.[40] For example, having an open medical staff, participating in Medicare and Medicaid, and treating all emergency patients without regard to ability to pay are common features of both tax-exempt and for-profit hospitals.

Although the focus of IRS policy is no longer the level of charity care that hospitals provide, the 1956 revenue ruling remains relevant, and IRS and various courts have continued to take into account the extent to which a hospital provides charity care when determining an organization's tax-exempt status. For example, among the factors that the Tax Court and several United States Courts of Appeals have considered in determining whether an organization met IRS's tax exemption requirements were existence of a charity care policy,[41] provision of free or below-cost services to individuals financially unable to make the required payments,[42] and provision of additional community benefit—other than making hospital services available to all in the community—that either further the function of government-funded institutions or would not likely be provided within the community without a hospital subsidy.[43]

State Community Benefit Requirements That Nonprofit Hospitals Must Meet Vary Substantially in Scope and Detail

State community benefit requirements that hospitals must meet in order to qualify for state tax-exempt or nonprofit status vary substantially in scope and detail. Specifically, 15 of the states have community benefit requirements in statutes or regulations and 36 do not (see Figure 2).[44] Of the 15 states with requirements, 5 states—Alabama, Mississippi, Pennsylvania, Texas, and West Virginia—specify a minimum amount of community benefits required in order for hospitals to be compliant with state requirements. Another 4 of the 15 states—Illinois, Indiana, Maryland, and Texas—have penalties for hospitals that fail to comply with their community benefit requirements.[45] Appendixes III, IV, V, VI, and VII contain more information on state community benefit requirements and other related provisions.

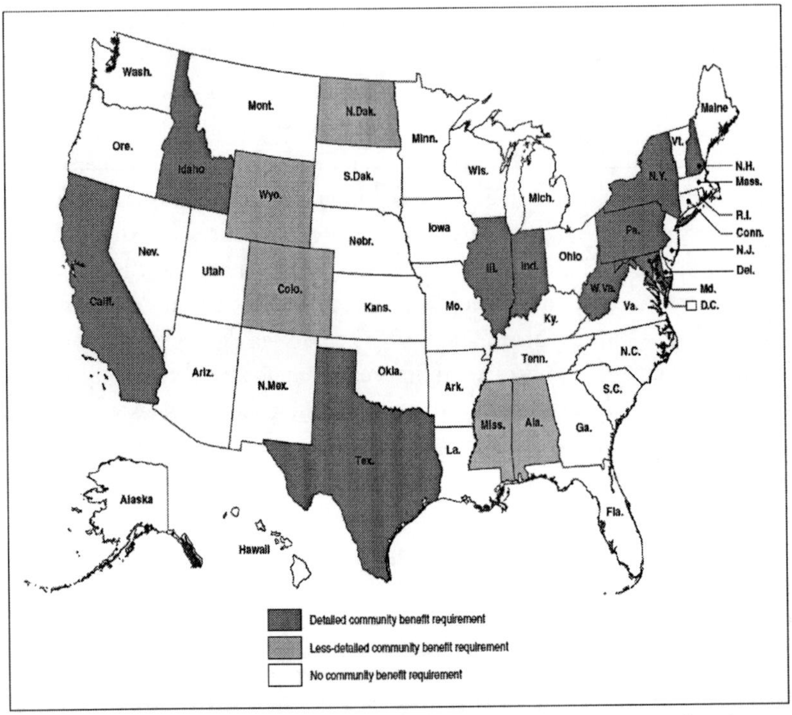

Sources: GAO analysis of state statutes and regulations; Map Resources (map).

Figure 2. State Community Benefit Requirements

In addition to the variation in scope among state community benefit requirements, the level of detail among such requirements also varies substantially. Specifically, of the 15 states with community benefit requirements, 10 states have detailed requirements and 5 states have less-detailed requirements.[46,47] The community benefit requirements of the 10 detailed states typically include some combination of the following factors: a definition of community benefit, requirements for a community benefit plan that sets forth how the hospital will provide community benefits, community benefit reporting requirements, and penalties for noncompliance. For example, California requires its nonprofit hospitals to adopt and annually update a community benefit plan, and annually submit a description of community benefit activities provided and their economic values, among other things.[48] Similarly, Illinois requires its hospitals to develop an organizational mission statement and a community benefits plan for serving the community's health care needs, and to submit an annual report of its community benefits plan, including a disclosure of the amount and types of community benefits actually provided.[49] These states also typically define community benefit using examples of, and guidance on, the types of activities considered to be community benefit. For example, Illinois defines community benefit using examples of activities that the state considers to be community benefit and Maryland defines community benefit using both examples and guidance.[50] In contrast, the remaining five states with less-detailed requirements either only require the provision of charity care or do not provide guidance on what counts as community benefit. For example, Alabama's requirement only provides that charity care must constitute at least 15 percent of a hospital's business in order for the hospital to be exempt from property tax; and Wyoming's requirement does not specify which activities its nonprofit hospitals must provide, but makes clear that hospitals must provide benefit to the community to obtain or maintain tax-exempt status.

DIFFERENCES IN THE ACTIVITIES NONPROFIT HOSPITALS DEFINE AS COMMUNITY BENEFIT SUBSTANTIALLY AFFECT THE AMOUNT OF COMMUNITY BENEFITS THEY REPORT

Variations in the activities nonprofit hospitals define as community benefit lead to substantial differences in the amount of community benefits they report. Among the government standards and industry guidance used by nonprofit hospitals, consensus exists to define many activities and their associated expenses—charity care, the unreimbursed cost of means-tested government programs, and many other activities that benefit the community—as community benefit. However, consensus does not exist to define bad debt and the unreimbursed cost of Medicare—each of which represents a substantial cost for nonprofit hospitals, according to the state data we analyzed—as community benefit.

Community Benefits May Include Charity Care, Bad Debt, Government Health Care Programs, and Other Activities That Benefit the Community

Activities that benefit the community and their associated expenses, as defined by the community benefit standards and guidance that nonprofit hospitals use, generally fall into one of four categories: charity care, care for patients whose accounts result in bad debt (referred to as bad debt for the rest of the report), care for beneficiaries of government health care programs and their associated unreimbursed costs, and other activities that benefit the community. In these standards and guidance, charity care is generally defined as care provided to patients whom the hospital deems unable to pay all or a portion of their bills. Bad debt is generally defined as the uncollectible payment that patients are expected to, but do not, pay. The unreimbursed cost of government health care programs is generally defined as the shortfall created when a facility receives total payments that are less than the total costs of caring for public program beneficiaries. Government health care programs include both means-tested programs for which eligibility is based on financial need, such as Medicaid, and nonmeans-tested programs for which eligibility is not based on financial need, such as Medicare. Lastly, other activities that benefit the community typically include activities that address a community need, and exclude activities that generate revenue for the hospital or are provided primarily for marketing purposes. These other activities generally fall into one of seven groups that the CHA and VHA guidance has identified, such as health professions education and medical research. Appendix II contains descriptions and examples of all seven groups.

While Consensus Exists to Define Charity Care as Community Benefit, Disagreement Exists over Bad Debt, Which Is a Substantial Cost for Nonprofit Hospitals

Consensus exists among the standards and guidance that nonprofit hospitals use to define charity care as community benefit. Specifically, among the five government and industry guidance documents we examined, four—IRS, AHA, CHA and VHA, and HFMA—define charity care as community benefit, as did all four state hospital associations we interviewed. While CMS does not have a position on community benefit, its reporting instrument collects information on uncompensated care and defines the term to include charity care.[51] In addition, of the 15 states with community benefit requirements, 14 either explicitly define community benefit to include charity care or, in the absence of a definition, mention charity care as an example of community benefit.

However, consensus does not exist among the standards and guidance that nonprofit hospitals use to define bad debt as community benefit. Among the five government and industry guidance documents we examined, two—CHA and VHA, and HFMA—specify that bad debt should not be defined as community benefit. CHA and VHA state that hospitals have the responsibility to better identify patients eligible for charity care, and thus distinguish charity care from bad debt.[52] Citing the difficulty of obtaining appropriate documentation to determine charity care eligibility, HFMA, while it does not define bad debt as community benefit, has stated that hospital charity care policies should address how to determine eligibility when patients do not provide sufficient information to formally make a determination.[53] In contrast, AHA defines bad debt as community benefit, as do three of the four state hospital associations we interviewed. AHA asserts that it should be defined as community benefit because the majority of bad debt is attributable to low-income patients who would qualify for charity care if hospitals were able to obtain the necessary documentation to formally make this determination.

Table 2. Charity Care and Bad Debt as Community Benefit—Analysis of Selected Government Agency and Industry Group Standards and Guidance

	Charity care	Bad debt
Government agencies		
CMS	O[a]	O[a]
IRS	√	O
Industry groups		
AHA	√	√
CHA/VHA	√	×
HFMA	√	×

√ Defined as community benefit

× Defined as not community benefit

O No position on whether to define as community benefit

[a] CMS does not have a position on community benefit; however, its reporting instrument collects information on uncompensated care and defines the term to include both charity care and bad debt.

IRS, on the other hand, has not taken a position on whether to define bad debt as community benefit (see table 2). The agency recognizes the divergence of practices and views in this area and, as stated by its officials, would like more information on the amount of bad debt attributable to low-income patients. As a result, IRS's community benefit reporting instrument—Form

990, Schedule H—will collect data on bad debt separately from the list of hospital activities that are traditionally included as community benefit, permit hospitals to explain why certain portions of bad debt should be defined as community benefit, and allow hospitals to estimate how much bad debt is attributable to low-income patients. CMS does not have a position on community benefit; however, its reporting instrument collects information on uncompensated care and defines the term to include bad debt. State community benefit requirements vary in whether they define bad debt as community benefit. Of the 15 states with community benefit requirements, 3 states explicitly include bad debt as community benefit, 2 states explicitly exclude bad debt, and 10 states do not specify.

Whether nonprofit hospitals define bad debt as community benefit has an important effect on the resulting amount of community benefit reported. Specifically, nearly all of the nonprofit hospitals in the four states we examined reported bad debt,[54] and the amounts were typically substantial when compared to charity care (see Figure 3). For example, in 2006 in California, the average percentage of total operating expenses devoted to bad debt was 7.4 percent—almost five times the average percentage devoted to charity care costs. Moreover, the amounts of hospitals' bad debt varied widely across hospitals. For example, among nonprofit hospitals in Texas, which had the most variation, the middle 50 percent of hospitals reported bad debt ranging from 7.4 to 19.1 percent of total operating expenses in 2006. Among the middle 50 percent of nonprofit hospitals in Massachusetts, which had the least variation, the span was still notable with bad debt ranging from 2.2 to 4.6 percent of total operating expenses in 2006.

While Consensus Exists to Define Means-Tested Programs, Such as Medicaid, as Community Benefit, the Unreimbursed Cost of Medicare, Which Is a Sizable Cost for Hospitals, Remains Contentious

Consensus exists among the standards and guidance nonprofit hospitals use to define the unreimbursed cost of means-tested government health care programs, such as Medicaid, as community benefit. Among the five government and industry guidance documents we examined, four—IRS, AHA, CHA and VHA, and HFMA—define the unreimbursed cost of such programs as community benefit, as did all four state hospital associations we interviewed. While CMS does not have a position on community benefit, its reporting instrument collects information on uncompensated care and includes the unreimbursed cost of such programs as a type of uncompensated care. In addition, state community benefit requirements generally include the unreimbursed cost of such programs as community benefit. Specifically, of the 15 states with community benefit requirements, 9 states explicitly include the unreimbursed cost of means-tested government health care programs as community benefit, none of the states explicitly exclude this cost, and 6 states do not specify.

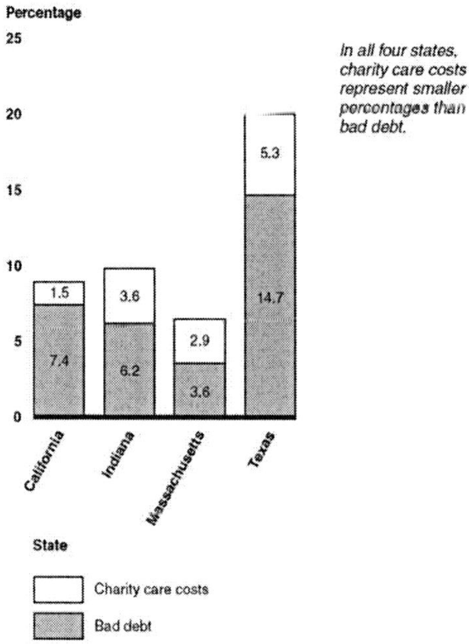

Source: GAO analysis of 2006 California, Indiana, Massachusetts, and Texas data.

Notes: Nonprofit hospitals include nongovernmental, acute care, general hospitals. Percentages are calculated only among those hospitals that reported having charity care costs and bad debt expenses. Ninety-six percent of hospitals in California, 81 percent of hospitals in Indiana, 97 percent of hospitals in Massachusetts, and 100 percent of hospitals in Texas reported charity care costs. Ninety-nine percent of hospitals in California, 99 percent of hospitals in Indiana, 97 percent of hospitals in Massachusetts, and 91 percent of hospitals in Texas reported bad debt.

Figure 3. Average Percentage of Total Operating Expenses Devoted to Charity Care Costs and Bad Debt among Nonprofit Hospitals in Selected States, 2006

Consensus does not, however, exist to define the unreimbursed cost of Medicare as community benefit. Among the five government agencies and industry groups we examined, only the CHA and VHA guidance specifies that the unreimbursed cost of Medicare should not be defined as community benefit because, among other reasons, Medicare losses for some hospitals may be associated with inefficiency and not underpayment.[55] CHA and VHA also note that all hospitals compete to attract Medicare beneficiaries, and CHA further stated that serving Medicare beneficiaries is not a differentiating feature of nonprofit hospitals.

In contrast, AHA defines the unreimbursed cost of Medicare as community benefit, and HFMA states that hospitals should decide, based on their circumstances, whether the unreimbursed cost of Medicare should be defined as community benefit.[56] AHA asserts that the unreimbursed cost of Medicare should be defined as community benefit because Medicare does not fully compensate hospitals for the cost of providing hospital care to Medicare beneficiaries. AHA also notes that Medicare, like Medicaid, serves a large number of low-income beneficiaries. HFMA states that the unreimbursed cost of Medicare can be an important issue for many providers and that such losses can be material to the facility's financial status; therefore, each hospital should decide, based on its circumstances, whether to report these costs as community benefit. Similarly, all four state hospital associations we interviewed stated that they define the unreimbursed cost of Medicare as community benefit.

IRS has not taken a position on whether to define the unreimbursed cost of Medicare as community benefit (see table 3). Its officials have stated that, similar to IRS's position on bad debt, IRS's community benefit reporting instrument will collect revenue and cost information related to hospitals' Medicare beneficiaries separately from the list of hospital activities that are traditionally included as community benefit, and permit hospitals to explain why they believe all or a portion of these costs should be defined as community benefit. CMS, which does not have a position on community benefit, does not collect information on the unreimbursed cost of Medicare. State community benefit requirements vary in whether the unreimbursed cost of Medicare should be included as community benefit. Of the 15 states with community benefit requirements, 6 states explicitly include the unreimbursed cost of Medicare as community benefit,[57] none of the states explicitly exclude this cost, and 9 states do not specify.

Whether nonprofit hospitals define the unreimbursed cost of Medicare as community benefit has an important effect on the resulting amount of community benefit reported. Specifically, most of the nonprofit hospitals in the four states we examined—over 90 percent in Texas and over 80 percent in California, Indiana, and Massachusetts—reported having unreimbursed costs of Medicare, and the amounts were typically substantial compared to charity care costs and the unreimbursed cost of Medicaid (see figure 4). For example, in all four states the unreimbursed cost of Medicare as a percentage of total operating expenses was at least 86 percent more than charity care costs as a percentage of the same expenses. Similarly, the unreimbursed cost of Medicare as a percentage of total operating expenses was at least 54 percent more than the unreimbursed cost of Medicaid as a percentage of the same expenses. Moreover, the amount of hospitals' unreimbursed cost of Medicare varied widely across hospitals. For example, among nonprofit hospitals in Indiana, which had the most variation, the middle 50 percent of hospitals reported unreimbursed costs of Medicare ranging from 4.9 to 13.4 percent of total operating expenses in 2006. Among the middle 50 percent of nonprofit hospitals in Massachusetts, which had the least variation, the span was still notable with unreimbursed costs of Medicare ranging from 2.4 to 8.0 percent of total operating expenses in 2006.

Table 3. Government Health Care Programs as Community Benefit—Analysis of Selected Government Agency and Industry Group Standards and Guidance

	Unreimbursed cost of means-tested government health care programs, such as Medicaid	Unreimbursed cost of Medicare program
Government agencies		
CMS	O[a]	O[a]
IRS	√	O
Industry groups		
AHA	√	√
CHA/VHA	√	×
HFMA	√	√[b]

Source: GAO analysis of government agency and industry group standards and guidance.

√ Defined as community benefit

× Defined as not community benefit

O No position on whether to define as community benefit

[a] CMS does not have a position on community benefit; however, its reporting instrument collects information on uncompensated care and includes the unreimbursed cost of means-tested government health care programs, but not Medicare, as a type of uncompensated care.

[b] HFMA asserts that hospitals should decide, based on their circumstances, whether the unreimbursed cost of Medicare should be defined as a community benefit.

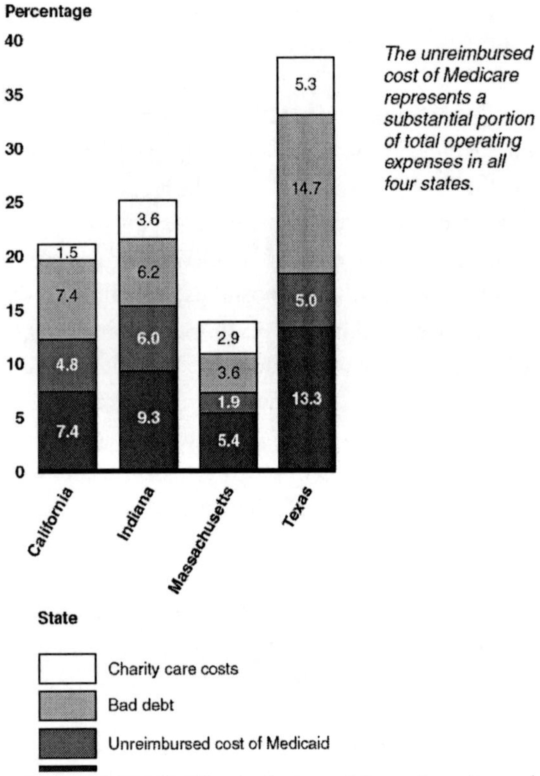

Source: GAO analysis of 2006 California, Indiana, Massachusetts, and Texas data.

Notes: Nonprofit hospitals include nongovernmental, acute care, general hospitals. Percentages are calculated only among those hospitals that reported having charity care costs, unreimbursed costs of Medicaid or Medicare, or bad debt expenses. Ninety-six percent of hospitals in California, 81 percent of hospitals in Indiana, 97 percent of hospitals in Massachusetts, and 100 percent of hospitals in Texas reported charity care costs. Ninety-nine percent of hospitals in California, 99 percent of hospitals in Indiana, 97 percent of hospitals in Massachusetts, and 91 percent of hospitals in Texas reported bad debt. Eighty-one percent of hospitals in California, 88 percent of hospitals in Indiana, 89 percent of hospitals in Massachusetts, and 87 percent of hospitals in Texas reported unreimbursed costs of Medicaid. Eighty-four percent of hospitals in California, 83 percent of hospitals in Indiana, 81 percent of hospitals in Massachusetts, and 93 percent of hospitals in Texas reported unreimbursed costs of Medicare.

Figure 4. Average Percentages of Total Operating Expenses Devoted to Charity Care Costs, Bad Debt, and the Unreimbursed Costs of Medicaid and Medicare among Nonprofit Hospitals in Selected States, 2006

Consensus Exists to Define Most Other Activities That Benefit the Community as Community Benefit

Consensus exists among the standards and guidance nonprofit hospitals use to define six of the seven groups of other activities as community benefit: cash and in-kind contributions,[58] community benefit operations,[59] community health improvement services,[60] health professions education,[61] medical research,[62] and subsidized health services.[63] State community benefit requirements on these activities vary. For example, 13 of the 15 states with community benefit requirements cite additional activities— other than charity care, bad debt, or government health care programs—as community benefit. For these states, the most commonly cited type of activity appears to be subsidized health services, although the exact term used varies among the states.

In contrast, consensus does not exist to define the seventh group of activities—community-building activities—as community benefit.[64] AHA, CHA and VHA, and HFMA define community-building activities as community benefit because these activities provide opportunities to address the underlying causes of health problems, such as poverty, homelessness, and environmental problems. IRS, however, has not taken a position on whether to define community-building activities, which include activities such as physical improvements and housing programs, economic development, and environmental improvements, as community benefit. The agency recognizes that there appears to be widespread support for including these activities, and while the agency believes that certain of these activities might constitute community benefit, more data and study are required. CMS also does not comment on what other activities should be defined as community benefit.

While data are not available to evaluate the effect of defining community-building activities as community benefit, data on groups of other activities that benefit the community indicate that they represent a relatively small proportion of total operating expenses for hospitals.[65] Only two of the four states we examined—Indiana and Texas—collect data on other activities that benefit the community, though even these states do not collect any data on two of the seven categories of other activities that benefit the community. For the five groups of other activities with data, fewer hospitals in Indiana and Texas generally reported having unreimbursed costs for these activities when compared with other types of community benefits, such as charity care, and the unreimbursed costs of most activities account for less than 1 percent each of total operating expenses, on average (see figure 5). For example, more hospitals in these two states reported having unreimbursed costs for community health improvement services than for the other four groups—over two-thirds of Indiana nonprofit hospitals and almost three-quarters of Texas nonprofit hospitals reported having these costs. Among Texas and Indiana nonprofit hospitals, the unreimbursed costs of these services averaged only 0.6 percent in 2006. In contrast, few hospitals reported having unreimbursed costs for medical research—less than 15 percent of nonprofit hospitals in both states reported these costs. Among Indiana nonprofit hospitals reporting these costs, the unreimbursed costs of medical research averaged only 0.1 percent of total operating expenses in 2006. In Texas, however, these costs averaged 0.8 percent, and the top quarter of hospitals had unreimbursed costs at least twice the average—at 1.7 percent in 2006.

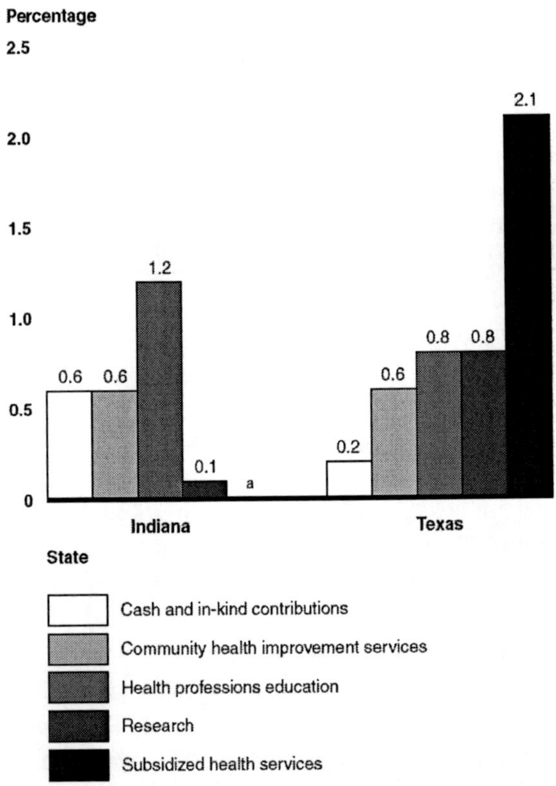

Source: GAO analysis of 2006 California, Indiana, Massachusetts, and Texas data.

Notes: Nonprofit hospitals include nongovernmental, acute care, general hospitals that reported these other activities. We did not include California and Massachusetts because they do not collect data on these activities. Percentages are calculated only among those hospitals that reported having unreimbursed costs of that activity. Cash and in-kind contributions to others include cash donations, grants, and in-kind donations made to individuals or the community at large. Community health improvement services include programs for community health education, community-based clinical services, and health care support services. Health professions education includes education for physicians, medical students, nurses, nursing students, and other health professionals, and scholarships and funding for professional education. Medical research includes both clinical and community-health research. Subsidized health services are clinical services provided despite a financial loss and subsidized by the hospital; examples include emergency services and burn units. Fifty percent of Texas hospitals reported unreimbursed costs of subsidized health services; Indiana does not collect data on these costs. Sixty-nine percent of Indiana hospitals and 75 percent of Texas hospitals reported unreimbursed costs of community health improvement services Fifty-four percent of Indiana hospitals and 60 percent of Texas hospitals reported unreimbursed costs of cash and in- kind contributions. Thirteen percent of Indiana hospitals and 9 percent of Texas hospitals reported unreimbursed costs of research. Fifty percent of Indiana hospitals and 58 percent of Texas hospitals reported unreimbursed costs of health professions education.

[a] Indiana does not collect data on subsidized health services.

Figure 5. Average Percentages of Total Operating Expenses Devoted to the Unreimbursed Costs of Other Activities That Benefit the Community among Nonprofit Hospitals in Selected States, 2006

In addition to representing a small proportion of total operating expenses, the costs of other activities that benefit the community are generally smaller than the costs of other types of activities that benefit the community, such as charity care, bad debt, and the unreimbursed costs of Medicaid and Medicare (see figure 6). For example, among nonprofit hospitals in Texas that incurred costs for providing other community benefits, the average cost of these activities—at 11 percent—is the smallest of the different groups of community benefits.

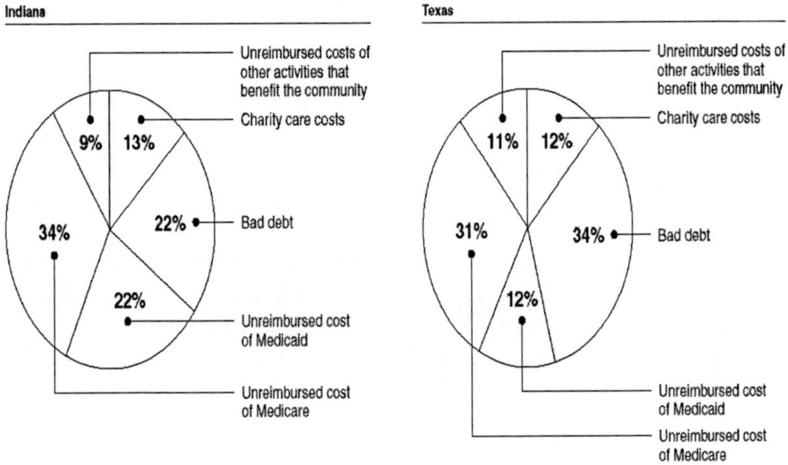

Source: GAO analysis of 2006 Indiana and Texas data.

Notes: Nonprofit hospitals include nongovernmental, acute care, general hospitals. We did not include California and Massachusetts because they do not collect data on other activities that benefit the community. Percentages are calculated only among those hospitals that reported having charity care costs; unreimbursed costs of Medicaid, Medicare, or other activities that benefit the community; or bad debt expenses. Other activities that benefit the community include cash and in-kind contributions to others, community health improvement services, health professions education, medical research, and subsidized health services. Eighty-one percent of hospitals in Indiana and 100 percent of hospitals in Texas reported charity care costs. Ninety-nine percent of hospitals in Indiana and 91 percent of hospitals in Texas reported bad debt. Eighty-eight percent of hospitals in Indiana and 87 percent of hospitals in Texas reported unreimbursed costs of Medicaid. Eighty-three percent of hospitals in Indiana and 93 percent of hospitals in Texas reported unreimbursed costs of Medicare. Fifty percent of Texas hospitals reported unreimbursed costs of subsidized health services; Indiana does not collect data on these costs. Sixty-nine percent of Indiana hospitals and 75 percent of Texas hospitals reported unreimbursed costs of community health improvement services. Fifty-four percent of Indiana hospitals and 60 percent of Texas hospitals reported unreimbursed costs of cash and in-kind contributions. Thirteen percent of Indiana hospitals and 9 percent of Texas hospitals reported unreimbursed costs of research. Fifty percent of Indiana hospitals and 58 percent of Texas hospitals reported unreimbursed costs of health professions education.

Figure 6. Charity Care Costs, Bad Debt, Unreimbursed Cost of Medicaid and Medicare, and Other Activities That Benefit the Community as Percentages of Their Sum among Nonprofit Hospitals in Selected States, 2006

Differences in How Nonprofit Hospitals Measure Costs of Community Benefit Activities Can Affect the Amount of Community Benefits They Report

Nonprofit hospitals may use a variety of practices to measure the costs of community benefit activities, and differences in these practices can affect the amount of community benefits they report. For example, standards and guidance used by nonprofit hospitals specify a variety of levels at which hospitals can report their community benefit. Specifically, IRS requires hospitals to report community benefit on Form 990 by employer identification number (EIN) because tax exemption is determined by EIN.[66] An EIN may cover a single hospital, several hospitals, or other aggregates. In contrast, CMS requires hospitals to submit cost reports, which include Worksheet S-10 with data on uncompensated care, at an individual hospital level. Industry stakeholders, such as AHA and CHA, have stated that hospitals should have the choice to report community benefits on a health care system level or as individual hospitals. CHA has stated that hospitals should have this option because, for example, they may also have established foundations or free health clinics as separate taxable entities through which they provide community benefit; hospitals should therefore have the option to include this community benefit in their reports. HFMA does not specify the level at which hospitals should report community benefit. The percentage of expenses devoted to community benefit could differ for hospitals that belong to a system depending on whether they reported at a system or individual level, because reporting at a system level aggregates the percentages of each hospital. One official from a state hospital association noted that because individual hospital percentages would be aggregated when community benefits are reported at a system level, there is a potential for a health care system as a whole, and not necessarily each individual hospital, to meet a community benefit standard.

Data are not available that would allow us to evaluate the impact of differences in the level at which nonprofit hospitals report community benefit. IRS's forthcoming Form 990, Schedule H, which will collect community benefit data, will be of limited use for comparing individual hospitals' reported community benefits because, as noted, hospitals may report community benefit as a single hospital or a larger aggregate, such as a health care system. CMS's Worksheet S-10 collects data on an individual hospital level, but we have found the data to be unreliable. MedPAC has stated that Worksheet S-10 should be improved, calling specifically for differentiating charity care and bad debt.[67,68] Although Worksheet S-10 could yield reliable data in the future, it does not currently collect data on all the activities IRS includes as community benefit, such as medical research or subsidized health services.

Standards and guidance used by nonprofit hospitals also differ in how they instruct hospitals to estimate costs of community benefit activities. Specifically, CHA and VHA and HFMA advocate calculating costs, if possible, using a cost-accounting system.[69] However, one state hospital association we spoke with stated that smaller hospitals may not be able to use this method. In contrast, CMS instructs hospitals to estimate costs on Worksheet S-10 using a cost-to-charge ratio (CCR).[70] CHA and VHA also suggest using a CCR when a cost-accounting system cannot be used. There are, however, many methods of calculating a CCR; CMS and CHA and VHA specify how hospitals should calculate the CCR used to determine charity care costs, but their formulas differ. AHA does not specify how to estimate costs, but supports the CHA and VHA guidance. IRS instructs hospitals to use a cost-accounting system, a CCR, or another cost-accounting method, whichever is most accurate in estimating costs. Data are not available that would allow us to evaluate the impact of the different practices hospitals use to estimate costs on the amount of reported community benefit.

In addition to the different practices on reporting levels and methodologies for estimating costs, which affect every aspect of reported community benefit, standards and guidance used by nonprofit hospitals also specify a variety of practices to measure the costs of charity care, government health care programs, and other activities that benefit the community, which can lead to inconsistent reporting of these activities.

Measurement Practices for Charity Care

Consensus does not exist on whether to add to charity care costs a nonprofit hospital's contributions to uncompensated care pools or programs,[71] or whether to offset charity care costs by payments to hospitals from uncompensated care pools or programs. AHA and CHA and VHA instruct hospitals to add their contributions and subtract the payments they receive to calculate charity care costs, but CMS and HFMA do not.[72] IRS instructs hospitals to account for revenue from uncompensated care pools or programs as offsetting either charity care costs, the unreimbursed cost of Medicaid, or both, depending on the state's primary purpose for the revenue. If the state's primary purpose is unclear, IRS instructs hospitals to allocate portions of the revenue as offsetting either charity care costs or the unreimbursed cost of Medicaid, based on a reasonable estimate of the portions that are intended for charity care and Medicaid.

Differences in how nonprofit hospitals calculate charity care costs can have an important effect on the resulting amount of community benefit a hospital reports. For nonprofit hospitals in Massachusetts in 2006,[73] the average percentage of total operating expenses devoted to charity care would increase from 2.9 to 3.9 percent—a 34 percent increase—if hospital contributions to uncompensated care pools were added to charity care costs. If payments Massachusetts hospitals receive from uncompensated care pools are then subtracted from the sum, the average percentage of total operating expenses devoted to charity care would decrease from 3.9 to 1.8 percent, a 54 percent reduction.

Measurement Practices for Government Health Care Programs

Consensus does not exist on how nonprofit hospitals are instructed to offset community benefit costs by Medicaid disproportionate share hospital (DSH) payments.[74] CHA and VHA specify that hospitals can account for these payments as offsetting either charity care costs or the unreimbursed cost of Medicaid. IRS instructs hospitals to account for Medicaid DSH payments as offsetting either charity care costs, the unreimbursed cost of Medicaid, or both depending on the state's primary purpose for the payment. If the state's primary purpose is unclear, IRS instructs hospitals to allocate portions of the payments as offsetting either charity care costs or the unreimbursed cost of Medicaid based on a reasonable estimate of the portions that are intended for charity care and Medicaid. CMS does not specify whether these payments should offset any specific costs. AHA and HFMA do not specify whether to include these payments, but support the CHA and VHA guidance.

Differences in how nonprofit hospitals calculate the unreimbursed cost of Medicaid can have an effect on the resulting amount of community benefit a hospital reports (see figure 7). For example, in Texas, the unreimbursed cost of Medicaid (5.0 percent of total operating expenses) is 32 percent more than the unreimbursed cost of Medicaid net of DSH payments (3.8 percent of total operating expenses). In Massachusetts, however, the unreimbursed cost of Medicaid is the same as the unreimbursed cost of Medicaid net of DSH payments—1.9 percent of total operating expenses.[75]

Moreover, consensus does not exist on whether nonprofit hospitals should add provider taxes, which are used to match funds for federal Medicaid resources, to the unreimbursed cost of Medicaid.[76] CHA and VHA instruct hospitals to include "Medicaid taxes" as a cost of Medicaid, describing these taxes as the provider fees that are used to match federal funds. In contrast, IRS instructs hospitals to account for these taxes as an element of charity care costs, the unreimbursed cost of Medicaid, or both, depending on the state's primary purpose for payments to hospitals from an uncompensated care pool or Medicaid DSH program. HFMA officials stated that provider taxes for Medicaid should be defined as community benefit because they are assessed for a means-tested program. CMS does not specify whether to include these taxes. AHA does not specify whether to include these taxes either, but supports the CHA and VHA guidelines. State data we obtained did not contain information that would allow us to analyze the impact of including these taxes as part of the unreimbursed cost of Medicaid.

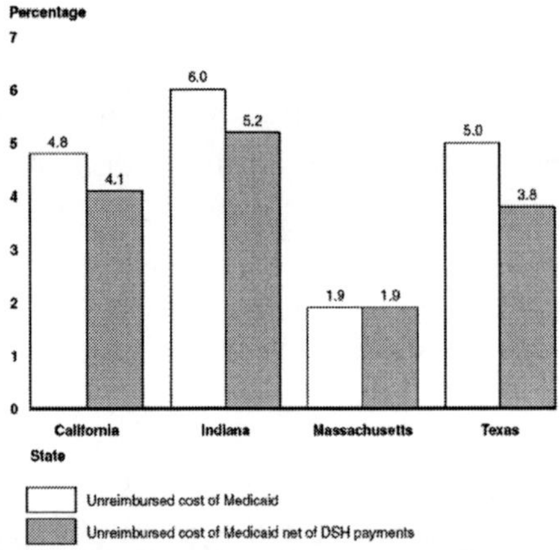

Source: GAO analysis of 2006 California, Indiana, Massachusetts, and Texas data.

Notes: Nonprofit hospitals include nongovernmental, acute-care, general hospitals. Medicaid provides health care coverage to eligible low-income people and is jointly financed by the federal government and the states. DSH payments are meant to compensate those hospitals that care for a disproportionate number of low-income patients. Average unreimbursed costs of Medicaid are calculated only among those hospitals that reported having unreimbursed costs of Medicaid: 81 percent of hospitals in California, 89 percent of hospitals in Indiana, 89 percent of hospitals in Massachusetts, and 87 percent of hospitals in Texas.

Figure 7. Average Percentages of Total Operating Expenses Devoted to the Unreimbursed Cost of Medicaid and to the Unreimbursed Cost of Medicaid Net of DSH Payments among Nonprofit Hospitals in Selected States, 2006

Measurement Practices for other Activities That Benefit the Community

While consensus exists to define most other activities as community benefit, the calculation of their costs using differing or nonexistent instructions may foster inconsistency. For example, the unreimbursed costs of subsidized health services may overlap with other reported community benefits. To account for this overlap, IRS, CHA and VHA, and HFMA specify that when reporting subsidized health services costs, hospitals should subtract the portion already counted as part of charity care costs and the unreimbursed costs of Medicaid. AHA does not specify whether these costs should be subtracted, but supports the CHA and VHA guidelines. CMS does not state which other activities it considers community benefit and therefore does not have guidance on measuring their costs. State data we obtained did not contain information that would allow us to analyze the effect of this overlap for measuring the cost of subsidized health services.

Concluding Observations

Since we last reported on the provision of uncompensated care by hospitals in 2005, both policymakers and the hospital industry have devoted considerable time and effort to the issue of community benefit. In particular, distinguishing between charity care and bad debt—two expenses that have historically been considered together as uncompensated care due to the difficulty of obtaining documentation necessary to distinguish patients unable to pay from those unwilling to pay—has emerged as a key technical issue whose resolution will go far in harmonizing positions in the policy debate.

With the added attention to community benefit has come a growing realization of the extent of variability among stakeholders in what should count and how to measure it. At the national level, in particular, there is substantial divergence of opinion on whether hospitals should be permitted to include bad debt and the unreimbursed cost of Medicare as community benefit. States vary considerably in the extent to which they have community benefit requirements, the nature of the requirements, and instructions on how to measure the components of community benefit. At present, determination and measurement of activities as community benefit for federal purposes are still largely matters of individual hospital discretion.

Given the large number of uninsured individuals, and the critical role of hospitals in caring for them, it is important that federal and state policymakers and industry groups continue their discussion addressing the variability in defining and measuring community benefit activities. An encouraging prospect for the future is the potential availability of two national data sources derived from mandatory reporting to IRS and CMS. National data should be helpful in standardizing reporting on community benefit activities and informing public policy on the community benefit standard. However, the data from these two sources will not be available for analysis for several years, and it remains to be seen whether the data will be consistent and reliable.

IRS Comments

IRS stated that the phrase "broad latitude to determine community benefit" overstates the looseness of the IRS standard and that such formulation is not supported by case law or published guidance. Specifically, IRS stated that the fact that hospitals may in practice exercise broad latitude does not make that the accepted IRS standard. In addition, IRS stated that the 1969 revenue ruling lists a specific set of factors, and court cases have closely followed the set of factors listed in that ruling. IRS stated that a correct characterization would be "some latitude" or "some flexibility," citing Geisinger Health Plan v. Comm'r, 985 F.2d 1210, 1217 (3rd Cir. 1993). We believe that because the standard affords considerable discretion to hospitals in both the determination and measurement of activities that demonstrate community benefit for federal purposes, the IRS standard allows nonprofit hospitals broad latitude to determine community benefit.

IRS commented that in the concluding observations section, the phrase "at present, determination and measurement of activities as community benefit for federal purposes are still largely matters of individual hospital discretion" was unclear as to whether the statement that follows "at present" refers to the state of things before or after IRS released the new Schedule H. IRS further stated that while in the years prior to IRS's Form 990, Schedule H, the determination and measurement of community benefit was largely a matter of individual hospital discretion, the new Schedule H provides clear standards. Specifically these clear standards cover (1) the types of activities reportable or not reportable as community benefit; (2) the fact that community benefit must be reported at cost rather than charges or otherwise; (3) the fact that community benefit must be reported by EIN (not by hospital or by system); and (4) the fact that bad debt, the unreimbursed cost of Medicare, and community-building activities cannot be included in the Part I quantifiable community benefit table, although they are reported elsewhere on Schedule H and IRS allows hospitals to explain what they think should count as community benefit. IRS stated that, going forward with Schedule H reporting requirements, there will be very little or no discretion regarding these measurement points. IRS further stated that the area where Schedule H provides individual organizations discretion is in whether the organization estimates the cost of community benefit activities using a CCR, a cost- accounting system, or a blend, so long as it is the most accurate information the organization has available. We believe that while Schedule H provides guidance with respect to the types of activities reportable as community benefit, it does not provide clear guidance on whether these activities do or do not count as community benefit for purposes of complying with IRS's community benefit standard. Schedule H indicates that bad debt, the unreimbursed cost of Medicare, and community-building activities cannot be included in the Part I quantifiable community benefit table; however, IRS has not clearly indicated whether it considers these items as counting toward meeting the community benefit requirement.

IRS noted that because its Form 990, Schedule H, requires reporting of bad debt and the unreimbursed cost of Medicare separately from items identified as community benefit, it is misleading to include these two items in the list along with charity care following the phrase "activities that benefit the community" because the phrase sounds like "community benefit," and Schedule H does not treat these items on par with Part I community benefit items such as charity care or unreimbursed cost of Medicaid. We agree with IRS's concern and have modified our text to clarify this distinction.

IRS stated that it would be an overstatement of the law to say uncategorically that a hospital need not meet all five factors to qualify for tax-exempt status.[77] IRS suggested that "the determination is based on all the facts and circumstances, and the absence of a particular factor may not necessarily be determinative," and cited the 1969 revenue ruling and IHC Health Plans, Inc. v. Comm'r, 325 F.3d 1188 (10th Cir. 2003). We agree with IRS's concern and have modified our text accordingly.

IRS also provided technical comments, which we incorporated as appropriate.

As agreed with your office, unless you publicly announce its contents earlier, we plan no further distribution of this chapter until 30 days after its issuance date. At the time, we will send copies to the Acting Administrator of CMS, the Commissioner of Internal Revenue, and interested congressional committees. We will also provide copies to others on request. The report is also available at no charge on GAO's Web site at http://www.gao.gov.

If you or your staff have any questions, please contact me at (202) 512-7114 or steinwalda@gao.gov. Contact points for our Offices of Congressional Relations and Public Affairs may be found on the last page of this chapter. GAO staff who made major contributions to this chapter are listed in appendix VIII.

Sincerely yours,

A. Bruce Steinwald
Director, Health Care

APPENDIX I: SCOPE AND METHODOLOGY

In conducting this study, we examined codified federal and state statutes and regulations. In addition, we analyzed state data on community benefits from California, Massachusetts, Indiana, and Texas. We selected these four states because they represent diverse areas geographically, and they collect data on nonprofit hospitals' community benefits, which not all states maintain.[78] We interviewed officials from the Internal Revenue Service (IRS) and the Centers for Medicare & Medicaid Services (CMS). We also interviewed representatives from the American Hospital Association (AHA); Association of American Medical Colleges; Catholic Health Association of the United States (CHA); Federation of American Hospitals; Healthcare Financial Management Association (HFMA); National Association of Children's Hospitals; VHA, Inc.; and state hospital associations and state health officials from California, Indiana, Massachusetts, and Texas. In addition, we interviewed representatives from seven nonprofit health care systems,[79] including health care systems in each of the four analyzed states that were referred to us by representatives from the state hospital associations.

To determine the community benefit standards IRS has established, we examined relevant provisions of the Internal Revenue Code, IRS regulations, revenue rulings, and federal case law. To review states' community benefit requirements, we defined "community benefit requirement" as a legal standard that expressly obligates a hospital to provide health care services or benefits to the community served by the hospital as a condition of maintaining tax-exempt status or qualifying as a nonprofit hospital. It is generally something that hospitals are required to do beyond their role of providing care for the sick and injured in exchange for remuneration or compensation. We considered the requirement to be one applicable to hospitals only if it either expressly referred to hospitals or expressly referred to care or services of the nature and type that one would reasonably expect to be provided by or performed primarily at acute care hospitals. We also limited our research concerning community benefit requirements to acute care, general hospitals. We looked only for codified state statutes and regulations that impose this type of requirement. If a statute or regulation described an activity that would fall into one of the commonly recognized "community benefit" categories identified by IRS, we considered it to present a community benefit activity.

We searched only for state statutes or regulations that require hospitals to perform relevant activities in order to maintain tax exemption or nonprofit status.[80] Thus, we excluded statutes and regulations that require hospitals to perform activities that benefit the community as a condition of obtaining hospital licensure, or that have the indirect effect of benefiting the community, such as state analogues to the Emergency Medical Treatment and Active Labor Act[81] and state vaccination provisions. We excluded standards that are very general, such as Hawaii's requirement that hospitals be "maintained to serve, and...do serve the public" in order to be exempt from property tax, although we did include requirements that specified that nonprofit hospitals do more than provide health care in exchange for compensation or remuneration. An example of the latter is Wyoming, which provides that "[t]he fundamental basis for [exemption from ad valorem taxation] is the benefit conferred upon the public by schools, orphan asylums and hospitals, and the consequent relief, to some extent, of the burden upon the state to educate, care and advance the interests of its citizens."

We limited our search to codified state statutes and regulations. In performing our search of state codes and regulations, we used some search terms, namely "community benefit," "charity care," "gift to the community," and "community service plan," but we did not limit our list of states with community benefit requirements to states that use only these terms. We then searched selected parts of state codes and administrative codes, limiting our search to the subject areas of hospitals, public health, tax, and corporations, to find community benefit requirements that do not use readily searchable terms. If we found one provision in a state code or regulation that imposed a community benefit requirement, we did not continue searching that state's authorities for additional or related provisions. Some state codes and regulations provided penalties for failing to comply with community benefit requirements. We noted penalty provisions only if the penalty provision made a direct and express reference to failure to comply with the community benefit requirement as the basis for the penalty.

We did not include in our scope state statutes and regulations that address community benefits but do not amount to requirements. These states include those whose statutes explicitly state that having a community benefits program is voluntary (Connecticut[82]) and those that require that hospitals report on the community benefits that they provide but do not actually require that they provide any community benefits (Connecticut,[83] Georgia,[84] Minnesota,[85] Nevada,[86] and Oregon[87]). Although we did not include these states in our count, we noted them in the report.

Due to our selection criteria, we included some states that organizations such as CHA, VHA, and Community Catalyst do not list in their compendia of states with community benefit laws, guidelines, and standards, and excluded some states that those organizations do include. We chose to use a broader definition of community benefit requirement, one that encompasses state statutes and regulations that may not use common community benefit terms, but nonetheless encompasses the same goals and types of activities as states that do use those terms. This reasoning led us to include Alabama, Colorado, Mississippi, North Dakota, and Wyoming.

We excluded provisions dealing with hospital conversions, mergers, or sales. These provisions often require that hospitals going through one of these processes take steps to ensure that levels of community benefits are maintained or safeguarded. We feel that such provisions should not be included in a general compendium of state community benefit requirements.[88] This means that we excluded some provisions that actually use the term "community benefit" and may even provide a detailed definition. We did this because such provisions apply in a limited context. They apply only to a limited number of hospitals (those that are going through conversion, merger, or sale), and they apply for a limited amount of time.

We excluded provisions granting tax exemption by merely incorporating by reference the standard contained in section 501(c)(3) of the Internal Revenue Code and provisions that used section 501(c)(3)-like language restricting nonprofit hospital activities. However, we did include provisions that by their language incorporated the 501(c)(3) standard and had a reporting requirement. An example of the latter is Idaho, which grants property tax exemption only to hospitals that have received tax exemption from IRS pursuant to section 501(c)(3).[89] In addition, Idaho hospitals granted tax exemption must annually submit a community benefits report.[90] An example of the former is Arizona, which grants tax exemption to organizations that are exempt from federal income tax.[91]

To examine what activities are defined as community benefits among the standards and guidance used by nonprofit hospitals, we reviewed the standards and guidance of federal agencies and industry groups.[92] To examine the effects of these standards and guidance on reported community benefit, we analyzed 2006 state data from California, Indiana, Massachusetts, and Texas. The state data were the most recent available at the time of our analysis. We limited our analysis to nonprofit, nongovernmental, acute care, general hospitals that reported gross patient revenues and total operating expenses. We calculated and compared a variety of hospital expenses, including charity care costs, bad debt, unreimbursed costs of government health care programs, and the costs of other activities that benefit the community, as percentages of total operating expenses. Charity care is generally defined as care provided to patients who the hospital deems unable to pay all or a portion of their bills. Bad debt is generally defined as the uncollectible payment that the patient is expected to, but does not, pay. The unreimbursed costs of government health care programs are generally defined as the shortfall created when a facility receives payments that are less than the costs of caring for public program beneficiaries. Other activities that benefit the community include health professions education and medical research. Not all of the four states we examined had data on all of these expenses, therefore, we calculated each expense as a percentage of total operating expenses whenever possible. We reduced charges to costs where possible in the data from all four states using cost-to-charge ratios. We did not reduce bad debt expenses because we found that hospitals did not consistently report bad debt in costs or charges.

To examine practices nonprofit hospitals use to measure community benefit activities, we reviewed the standards and guidance from IRS, CMS, AHA, CHA and VHA, and HFMA. To examine the effects of these practices on reported community benefit, we analyzed 2006 state data from California, Indiana, Massachusetts, and Texas. We compared the different ways hospitals calculate expenses, including charity care costs and the unreimbursed cost of Medicaid,[93] as percentages of total operating expenses. Not all of the four states had data to compare the different practices to measure all of these expenses; therefore, we calculated each expense as a percentage of total operating expenses whenever possible.

We assessed the reliability of the state data from California, Indiana, Massachusetts, and Texas in two ways. First, we performed tests of data elements for all four states. For example, we examined the values for total operating expenses and gross patient revenues to determine whether these data were complete and reasonable. Second, we interviewed state officials knowledgeable about the data and reviewed documentation related to the data. We determined that all four states employed various data consistency checks, including outlier and trend analysis and targeted follow-up with hospitals on a case-by-case basis, to assess the quality of the data they collected. We determined that the data we used in our analyses were sufficiently reliable for our purposes.

We conducted our work from July 2007 through August 2008 in accordance with generally accepted government auditing standards.

We assessed the reliability of the state data from California, Indiana, Massachusetts, and Texas in two ways. First, we performed tests of data elements for all four states. For example, we examined the values for total operating expenses and gross patient revenues to determine whether these data were complete and reasonable. Second, we interviewed state officials knowledgeable about the data and reviewed documentation related to the data. We determined that all four states employed various data consistency checks, including outlier and trend analysis and targeted follow-up with hospitals on a case-by-case basis, to assess the quality of the data they collected. We determined that the data we used in our analyses were sufficiently reliable for our purposes.

We conducted our work from July 2007 through August 2008 in accordance with generally accepted government auditing standards.

APPENDIX II: OTHER ACTIVITIES THAT BENEFIT THE COMMUNITY IDENTIFIED IN INDUSTRY GUIDANCE

Groups of other activities that benefit the community[a]	Description	Examples of activities included in the group	Examples of activities not included in the group
Cash and in-kind contributions	Donations and grants provided to individuals or the community at large, and fundraising for community programs.	• Contributions provided to charity events and individuals for emergency assistance. • Program, operating, and education grants; matching grants; and event sponsorship. • Meeting room overhead and space for nonprofit or community groups, emergency medical care at a community event, and provision of facility parking vouchers for patients and families in need. • Grant writing and other fundraising efforts specific to community programs.	• Employee-donated funds and fees for sporting event tickets. • Employee community involvement when activities are on employees' own time and volunteer hours by employees on own time.
Community benefit operations	Community benefit strategic planning and operations.	• Staff costs to coordinate community benefit volunteer programs. • Community health needs assessment and community asset assessments, such as a youth asset survey.	• Volunteer time of individuals for community benefit volunteer programs. • Market share assessment or marketing survey process.

Appendix (Continued)

Community-building activities	Activities intended to enhance the development of	• Community gardens, neighborhood improvement, and revitalization projects.	• Housing for employees and health facility construction and
	community health programs and partnerships.	• Small business development and participation in an economic development council or chamber of commerce. • Neighborhood watch groups and child care for community residents with qualified need. • Lead or radon programs and efforts to reduce community environmental hazards. • Training in conflict resolution, cultural skills, civics skills, or language skills, and community leadership development. • Hospital representation at community coalitions. • Local, state, and national advocacy related to access to health care and public health issues. • Recruitment of health professionals for areas identified by the government as medically underserved.	improvements, such as a meditation garden or parking lot. • Routine financial investments. • Routine and mandated disaster preparedness. • Interpreter training programs for hospital staff as required by law. • Advocacy specific to hospital operations and financing. • Programs that address only the workforce needs of the health care organization rather than community-wide issues.

Community health improvement services	Programs for community health education, community-based clinical services, and health care support services.	• Prenatal and childbirth classes serving at-risk and low-income persons, public service announcements with health messages, support groups, and self-help programs. • Screenings, one-time or occasionally held clinics, clinics for underinsured and uninsured persons, and mobile units used to deliver primary care services. • Information and referrals to community services and assistance with enrollment in government health care programs.	• Health education classes designed to increase market share, support given to patients and families in the course of their hospital visits, and employee wellness and health promotion provided as an employee benefit. • Screenings provided primarily for public relations or marketing, screenings and clinics for which a fee is charged and a profit is realized, volunteers' time, and mobile units that provide specialty care that is an extension of the hospital's outpatient department. • Routine discharge planning and enrollment assistance services designed to increase facility revenue.

Appendix (Continued)

<table>
<tr><td>Health professions education</td><td>Education for physicians, medical students, nurses, nursing students, and other</td><td>• Internships, clerkships, and residencies.
• Providing a clinical setting for undergraduate training or vocational training to students</td><td>• Continuing medical education restricted to members of the medical staff.
• Education required of</td></tr>
<tr><td></td><td>health professionals, and scholarships and funding for professional education.</td><td>enrolled in an outside organization, and the costs of high school student job shadowing and mentoring projects.
• Nursing scholarships or tuition payments for professional education to non-employees and volunteers.</td><td>nursing staff and staff time spent delivering care that is concurrent with job shadowing.
• Tuition reimbursement provided as an employee benefit.</td></tr>
<tr><td>Medical research</td><td>Clinical and community-health research to be shared with persons outside the organization.</td><td>• Research development, using formal research protocols; studies on therapeutic protocols; evaluation of innovative treatments; and research papers prepared by staff for professional journals.
• Studies on health issues for vulnerable persons, community health, and innovative health care delivery models.</td><td>• Research where findings are used only internally.</td></tr>
</table>

Subsidized health services	Clinical services provided despite a financial loss, even after removing the effects of charity care and unreimbursed cost of Medicaid. If no longer offered, these services would either be unavailable in the area or fall to the responsibility of government or another nonprofit organization.	• Subsidies provided to maintain the availability of these clinical services. • Emergency and trauma services, neonatal intensive care, burn units, women's and children's services, renal dialysis services, subsidized continuing care, behavioral health services, and palliative care.	• Charity care, bad debt, and unreimbursed cost of Medicaid. • Services provided in order to attract physicians or health plans. • Routine pain control program.

Source: Catholic Health Association of the United States, *A Guide for Planning and Reporting Community Benefit* (St. Louis, 2006).

[a] Activities that benefit the community, as defined by the standards and guidance used by nonprofit hospitals, generally fall into one of four categories: charity care, bad debt, unreimbursed costs of government health care programs, and other activities that benefit the community.

APPENDIX III: STATE COMMUNITY BENEFIT REQUIREMENTS

As of March 2008, 15 states require that hospitals provide community benefits in order to receive tax exemption or achieve nonprofit status. However, state community benefit requirements[94] vary greatly in scope and level of detail (see app. IV).[95]

States with Detailed Community Benefit Requirements

Of the 15 states with community benefit requirements, 10 have detailed community benefit requirements.[96] We considered states to provide a "detailed" definition if they provided some combination of the following: a definition of community benefit, requirements for a community benefits plan that sets forth how the hospital will provide community benefits, reporting requirements, and penalties for noncompliance. These states typically set forth a detailed definition of community benefit, specifying numerous categories of activities that qualify, and are consistent with the level of detail of community benefit definitions used by the Catholic Health Association of the United States and other similar entities (see app. II). Illinois, for example, includes the unreimbursed cost of providing charity care, language assistant services, government-sponsored indigent health care, donations, volunteer services, education, government- sponsored program services, research, subsidized health services, and collecting bad debts.[97] Illinois specifically excludes the cost of paying taxes or other governmental assessments. Maryland defines community benefit as "an activity that is intended to address community needs and priorities primarily through disease prevention and improvement of health status, including... [h]ealth services provided to vulnerable or underserved populations such as Medicaid, Medicare, or Maryland Children's Health Program enrollees... [f]inancial or in kind support of public health programs...[d]onations of funds, property, or other resources that contribute to a community priority... [h]ealth care cost containment activities; and... [h]ealth education, screening, and prevention services."[98]

These 10 states also tend to have very detailed instructions on how community benefits should be provided and reported. They may include a description of the required elements of and the process by which a hospital should compose its community benefits plan and the required elements to be provided in a hospital's annual report to the relevant authority. A typical example is California, which requires each of its nonprofit hospitals to have a mission statement that requires that hospital's policies to integrate and reflect the public interest in meeting its responsibilities as a nonprofit organization; complete a community needs assessment in consultation with community groups and government officials; update its community needs assessment every 3 years; adopt and annually update a community benefits plan for providing community benefits either alone or in conjunction with other entities; and annually submit its community benefits plan, including a description of the activities undertaken and the economic value of community benefits provided.[99]

Other States with Community Benefit Requirements

The remaining five states with community benefit requirements have provisions that are less detailed.[100] Alabama requires that charity care constitute at least 15 percent of a hospital's business in order for it to be exempt from property tax.[101] Wyoming provides that "[t]he fundamental basis for [exemption from ad valorem taxation] is the benefit conferred upon the public by schools, orphan asylums and hospitals, and the consequent relief, to some extent, of the burden upon the state to educate, care and advance the interests of its citizens."[102] States such as Wyoming do not specify activities that their nonprofit hospitals must provide, but their provisions make clear that, in order to receive tax exemption or achieve nonprofit status, hospitals must provide benefit to the community. In contrast to the 10 detailed states, these 5 states typically either require the provision of a certain amount of charity care without mentioning other categories of community benefit or do not give guidance as to what counts as a community benefit. For the latter states, such as Wyoming, it is not always clear what types of community benefit activities would fulfill a hospital's obligations.

States without Community Benefit Requirements

The remaining 36 states do not have community benefit requirements in codified statutes or regulations that hospitals must meet to qualify for tax-exempt or nonprofit status. Among these states are three groups of states that address community benefit in some way but do not have "community benefit requirements" as we define that term. Some states apply their community benefits provisions to all hospitals, such as in the context of hospital licensure, rather than to tax exemption or nonprofit status (see app. V). Examples of states that fall into this category are Massachusetts, New Mexico, and Rhode Island, and they require all hospitals, both for- profit and nonprofit, to provide some form of community benefits. A second group requires that hospitals periodically report to the relevant authority the community benefits that they provide but do not require that hospitals actually provide any community benefits (see app. VI).[103] A third group discusses community benefit in sources other than codified statutes or regulations, such as attorney general guidelines or property tax exemption standards (see app. VII). One state, Utah, discusses community benefit in a set of standards of practice for property tax exemptions and through its case law.[104] Although Massachusetts has a statute requiring community benefits for licensure purposes, the bulk of its community benefit discussion is found in a set of attorney general guidelines.[105] We did not include these groups of states in our count of states with community benefit requirements, and we provide information on these states as examples rather than as the product of a comprehensive analysis of state sources.

Penalties

Hospitals may be penalized if they fail to comply with community benefit requirements. Of the 15 states with community benefit requirements, 4 have explicit penalties for failure to comply and 11 states do not specify a penalty.[106] Examples of states with explicit penalties include Indiana, Maryland, and Texas, where civil penalties may be assessed against nonprofit hospitals that fail to submit their annual reports in a timely fashion.[107] Of the 11 states that do not specify a penalty, if the requirement is tied to tax exemption, a nonprofit hospital could be denied tax exemption for a period of time.

For states without community benefit requirements but with community benefit provisions tied to hospital licensure requirements, a hospital that has not complied with the community benefit provisions will not be licensed (or its license may be suspended or revoked).[108] In addition, states may include explicit penalties for failure to comply with community benefit provisions tied to hospital licensure requirements. For example, in Rhode Island, a state that applies its community benefits provisions to all hospitals through licensure requirements, failure to comply with statewide standards for community benefits may result in criminal penalties: the Superior Court may, after notice and opportunity for a prompt and fair hearing, impose a prison term of up to 5 years for a person who knowingly violates or fails to comply with the requirements or willingly or knowingly gives false or incorrect information in connection with its licensure requirements.[109]

Quantity

Most states do not specify a minimum quantity of community benefits that must be provided in order to satisfy requirements. Five states require that hospitals provide a specified amount of community benefit.[110] Alabama requires that "[t]o be exempt from ad valorem taxation, the treatment of charity patients must constitute at least 15 percent of the business of the hospital,"[111] while Texas requires that its hospitals comply with one or more of three standards: a level reasonable in relation to community needs; at least 100 percent of its tax-exempt benefits, excluding federal income tax; or at least 5 percent of its net patient revenue (in which case charity care and government-sponsored indigent care must be at least 4 percent of net patient revenue).[112] In other states, the required minimum quantity is not a specified dollar amount or percentage. For example, Mississippi requires that, to be exempt from property tax, hospitals must maintain at least one ward for charity patients.[113] West Virginia requires that charitable hospitals provide free and below-cost necessary medical services in an amount determined by their boards of trustees consistent with their ability to do so.[114]

In addition to states that specify a minimum quantity of community benefits that must be provided in order to satisfy community benefit requirements, the remaining states—those without minimum quantity requirements and those without community benefit requirements as we define that term—tend to require the submission of community benefits plans, annual reports, or both to relevant state authorities. Even without an explicit requirement to provide community benefits, these provisions may bring a measure of accountability as to quantity, since relevant authorities have an opportunity to review hospital activities. An example of a state without a minimum quantity requirement is California, which provides that hospitals must annually report on the economic value of community benefits provided in furtherance of their community benefits plans.[115]

Appendix IV: States with Community Benefit Requirements Related to Hospitals

State	Description of requirements	Activities included in the definition of community benefit	Penalties
Alabama	To be exempt from ad valorem taxation on property up to $75,000, the treatment of charity patients must constitute at least 15 percent of the business of the hospital. (Ala. Code § 40-9-1)	• Charity. (Ala. Code § 40-9-1)	None specified.
California	1. Update community needs assessment at least once every 3 years. 2. Annually adopt and update a community benefits plan, including mechanisms to evaluate its effectiveness, measurable objectives, and community benefits categorized into a specified framework. 3. Annually submit the community benefits plan, including activities undertaken and economic value of community benefits provided. (Cal. Health & Safety Code §§ 127350, 127355)	• Charity care and unreimbursed costs of health care services. • Community-oriented wellness and health promotion services. • Prevention service (screenings, immunizations, disease counseling, education). • Adult day care and child care. • Medical research and medical education. • Nursing and other professional training. • Home-delivered meals to the homebound. • Sponsorship of free food, shelter, and clothing to the homeless. • Outreach clinics in socioeconomically depressed areas. • Financial or in-kind support of public health programs. • Donations that contribute to a community priority. • Health care cost containment. • Enhancement of access to health care. • Services offered without regard to financial return • Goods or services that help maintain a person's health. (Explicitly not limited to this list of activities.) (Cal. Health & Safety Code § 127345)	None specified.
Colorado	Property must be owned and used solely and exclusively for strictly charitable purposes. (Colo. Rev. Stat. Ann. § 39-3-108)	• A gift for the benefit of an indefinite number of persons by relieving their bodies from disease, by assisting them to establish them selves in life, or by erecting or maintaining public buildings or works, or otherwise	None specified.

State	Description of requirements	Activities included in the definition of community benefit	Penalties
		lessening the burdens of government. (8 Colo. Code Regs. 1304-2)	
Idaho	1. Show that the hospital is organized as a nonprofit corporation in Idaho or another state and has received an exemption from taxation from IRS pursuant to § 501(c)(3) of the Internal Revenue Code. 2. Exempt hospitals with at least 150 patient beds must prepare and file an annual community benefits report that itemizes the community benefits provided and indicates the process the hospital used to determine general community needs. (Idaho Code § 63-602D)	• Charity care. • Bad debt. • Under-reimbursed care covered through government programs. • Services and programs provided below actual cost. • Donated time, funds, subsidies, and in-kind services. • Additions to capital. (Idaho Code § 63-602D)	None specified.
Illinois	1. Organization mission statement. 2. Community benefits plan. 3. Annual report of the community benefits plan. 4. Statement noting that the annual report is public information. 5. Provide the report as a matter of community information. (210 Ill. Comp. Stat. 76/15, 76/20)	• Charity care. • Language assistant services. • Government-sponsored indigent health care. • Donations. • Volunteer services. • Education. • Government-sponsored program services. • Research. • Subsidized health services. • Bad debt. Does not include the cost of paying taxes or other governmental assessments. (210 Ill. Comp. Stat. 76/10)	The Attorney General may assess a late filing fee against a nonprofit hospital that fails to file the annual report. The fee must not exceed $100; the Attorney General may grant extensions for good cause. (210 Ill. Comp. Stat. 76/25) Other rights and remedies available to the state are retained. (210 Ill. Comp. Stat. 76/30)

(Continued)

Indiana	1. Organization mission statement. 2. Community benefits plan.	• Charity care. • Government-sponsored indigent health care.	The state department may assess a civil penalty against a nonprofit
	3.Communitywide needs assessments in aid of community benefits plan. 4.Annual report of the community benefits plan. 5.Statement notifying the public that the annual report is public information. 6.Written notice about charity care program. (Ind. Code §§ 16-21-9-4, -5, -6, -7)	• Donations. • Education. • Government-sponsored program services. • Research. • Subsidized health services. Does not include the cost of paying taxes or other governmental assessments. (Ind. Code § 16-21-9-1)	hospital that fails to submit its annual report. The penalty may not exceed $1,000 for each day a reportis late. (Ind. Code § 16-21-9-8)
Maryland	1. Identify community health care needs. 2. Annual community benefits report, which includes the hospital's mission statement, a list and costs of each community benefit initiative, a description of efforts undertaken to evaluate the effectiveness of each initiative, and a description of gaps in availability of specialist providers to serve the uninsured. (Md. Code Ann., Health-Gen. § 19-303)	• Health services provided to vulnerable or underserved populations, such as Medicaid, Medicare, or Maryland Children's Health Program enrollees. • Financial or in-kind support of public health programs. • Donations that contribute to a community priority. • Health care cost containment activities. • Health education, screening, and prevention services. (Md. Code Ann., Health-Gen. § 19-303)	For failure to file the community benefits report: civil penalty of $100 per day unless an extension is granted. The Health Services Cost Review Commission may refuse to grant a rate increase to any hospital that does not file a required report. Any substantially incomplete or inaccurate report may not be considered timely filed. Institutions may request reasonable extensions of time to file required reports. (Md. Regs. Code tit. 10, § 37.01.03)

Mississippi	Must maintain one or more charity wards for charity patients (Miss. Code Ann. § 27-31-1(f))	• Charity. (Miss. Code Ann. § 27-31-1)	None specified.
New Hampshire	1. Annual report of community benefits plan, which includes a mission statement, community needs assessment, community benefit activities expected to be undertaken or supported, community benefit activities undertaken in the previous year and a	• Charity care. • Financial or in-kind support of public health programs, including support of recommendations in any state health plan. • Allocation of resources that promote or support a healthier community, enhanced access to health care or related services, health education and prevention	None specified.
	description of results or outcomes, means used to solicit community views, an evaluation of the plan's effectiveness, an estimate of the cost of each activity expected, and a report on the unreimbursed cost of activities undertaken in the previous year. 2. Community needs assessment. 3. Make the community benefits plan available to the public. (N.H. Rev. Stat. Ann. §§ 7.32-e, -f, -g)	activities, or services to a vulnerable population. • Medical research and education and training of health care practitioners, including the pooling of funds with other providers. (Explicitly not limited to the listed activities.) (N.H. Rev. Stat. Ann. § 7.32-d)	

(Continued)

New York	1.Issue an organizational mission statement. 2.At least every 3 years: • review and amend the mission statement, • solicit community views, • demonstrate operational and financial commitment to meeting community health care needs, and • prepare and make available to the public a statement of the hospital's financial resources and allocation to hospital purposes, including the provision of free or reduced charge services. 3. Annually prepare and make available to the public an implementation report. 4. File with the Commissioner of Health its mission statement, annual implementa-tion report, and 3-year report. (N.Y. Pub. Health Law § 2803-l)	• Meeting community health care needs. • Charity care. • Improving access to health care services by the underserved. (N.Y. Pub. Health Law § 2803-l)	None specified.
North Dakota	To receive sales and use tax exemptions, must be organized and operated exclusively in providing services for the purposes of preventing and alleviating human illness and injury. (N.D. Cent. Code §§ 57-39.2-04, 57-40.2-04)	• Education. • Research. • Community service. • Direct patient services, income being derived solely from private donations with some exceptions of a minimal membership fee. (N.D. Cent. Code §§ 57-39.2-04, 57-40.2-04)	None specified.

Pennsylvania	1 Must advance a charitable purpose. 2. Must donate or render gratuitously a substantial portion of its services. 3. Must benefit a substantial and indefinite class of persons who are legitimate subjects of charity. 4. Must relieve the government of some of its burden. (10 Pa. Cons. Stat. § 375)	• Charity care. • Goods or services to individuals eligible for government programs. • Donations to institutions of purely public charity or government agencies. • Uncompensated goods or services, including the difference between full cost and fee received for all goods or services provided, education and research programs, and unreimbursed costs of government programs, including Medicare and Medicaid, and unreimbursed community services. • Reasonable value of volunteer assistance. • Cost of goods or services provided to individuals who are unable to pay, provided that reasonable and customary collection efforts have been made. • Services to the public that directly or indirectly reduce dependence on government programs or relieve or lessen the burden borne by government for the advancement of social, moral, educational, or physical objectives. (10 Pa. Cons. Stat. § 375)	None specified.
Texas	1.Provide health care services to thecommunity. 2.Comply with all federal, state, and local government requirements for tax exemption in order to maintain such	• Charity care. • Government-sponsored indigent health care. • Donations. • Education. • Government-sponsored program services.	A nonprofit hospital that fails to make a report of the community benefits plan is subject to a civil penalty not exceeding $1,000 per day. No penalty may be assessed against a hospital

(Continued)

	exemption. 3. Provide a specified minimum amount of community benefits. 4. Admission policy must provide for the admission of financially indigent and medically indigent persons. 5. Organizational mission statement. 6. Community benefits plan. 7. Communitywide needs assessments to develop the community benefits plan. 8. Annual report of the community benefits plan, including amount and types of community benefits provided. (Tex. Health & Safety Code Ann. §§ 311.043, 311.044, 311.045)	• Research. • Subsidized health services. Does not include the cost of paying taxes or other governmental assessments. (Tex. Health & Safety Code Ann. § 311.042; 25 Tex. Admin. Code § 13.13)	until 10 business days have elapsed after written notification to the hospital of its failure to file a report. (Tex. Health & Safety Code Ann. §§ 311.047, 311.048) 1. Subject to a civil penalty of not more than $1,000 for each dayof noncompliance. 2. If a nonprofit hospital/system does not submit a report of the community benefits plan within the established reporting period, the Department of Health may institute the following procedures: A. Notify the entity that it is in noncompliance with the Department of Health's reporting requirements and that the

			Commissioner of Health may request that the Attorney General institute and conduct a suit in the name of the state to recover civil penalties if the hospital fails to submit the report to the Department of Health within 10 days of receipt of the letter. B. If the Department of Health does not receive the report of the community benefits plan from the nonresponding hospital within the specified time frame, the Commissioner of Health may notify the Attorney General in

(Continued)

			writing of the entity's noncompliance. The Department of Health will send a copy to the hospital. (25 Tex. Admin. Code § 13.18)
West Virginia	1. Must provide an amount of free and below-cost necessary medical services as determined by its board of trustees, consistent with other provisions, to those who are unable to pay. 2. Charitable use (determined by an examination of several factors, including charity care, promotion of health, relief of burdens of government, and volunteer and community services). 3. Charity care plan that reflects specified minimum criteria. 4. Review charity care plan not less than every 2 years. (W. Va. Code St. R. § 110-3-24)	• Charity care. • Activities that promote the health of the community and/or decrease the burdens of state, county, and municipal governments. • Shortfall between approved charges and payments received from Medicaid and similar governmental programs. • Volunteer and community services. • Public education programs. • Donations. • Free, low-cost, or below-cost health screenings and assessments. • Social services assistance/counseling. • Free or reduced-charge medical clinics. • Operation of poison control centers. • Free or below-cost blood banking services. • Free or below-cost assistance, material, equipment and training to emergency medical services and ambulance services. • Disaster planning. • Unreimbursed costs for education and training. (W. Va. Code St. R. § 110-3-24)	None specified.

Wyoming	1. The fundamental basis for ad valorem tax exemption is the benefit conferred upon the public and the consequent relief, to some extent, of the burden	• Benefit conferred upon the public. • Consequent relief of the burden upon the state. • Indigent care. • Promote health care.	None specified.
	upon the state to educate, care, and advance the interests of its citizens. Such institutions thus confer a benefit upon the general citizenry of the state and render an essential service for which they are relieved of certain burdens of taxation. 2. Indigent care shall be afforded through admission to the institution based on the clinical judgment of the physician, not upon the patient's financial ability or inability to pay. (Wyo. Stat. Ann. § 39-11-105; Wyo. R. & Regs. Rev Gen Ch. 14 § 10)	• Provide health-related assistance to the general public. (W.S. 1977 § 39-11-105; Wyo. R. & Regs. Rev Gen Ch. 14 § 10)	

Source: GAO analysis of Alabama, California, Colorado, Idaho, Illinois, Indiana, Maryland, Mississippi, New Hampshire, New York, North Dakota, Pennsylvania, Texas, West Virginia, and Wyoming statutes and regulations.

Notes: We did not consider loss of tax exemption to be a penalty. We considered only those states whose statutes or regulations require the provision of community benefits for purposes of tax exemption or nonprofit status to have community benefit requirements.

Appendix V: Examples of States with Licensure-Related Community Benefit Provisions

State	Description of requirements	Activities included in the definition of community benefit	Penalties
Massachusetts	Applicants for a license to establish or maintain an acute-care hospital must agree to maintain or increase the percentage of revenues allocated to free care and submit a plan for the provision of community benefits. (Mass. Gen. Laws Ann. ch. 111, § 51G)	• Identification and provision of essential health services. • Primary and preventive health care services. (Mass. Gen. Laws Ann. ch. 111, § 51G)	None specified.
New Mexico	1. Acute-care or general hospitals can be licensed only if they agree to provide emergency services and general health care to nonpaying patients and low-income reimbursed patients in the same proportion as the patients are treated in acute-care general hospitals in the local community. The annual cost of this care shall not exceed 5 percent of the hospital's annual revenue. 2. These hospitals must annually report the cost of care for emergency and general health care to nonpaying and low-income reimbursed patients and the number of nonpaying and low-income reimbursed patients treated. (N.M. Stat. Ann. § 24-1-5.8(C); N.M. Admin. Code tit. 7, § 7.2.8)	• Emergency services and general health care provided to nonpaying patients and low-income reimbursed patients. (N.M. Stat. Ann. § 24-1-5.8(C); N.M. Admin. Code tit. 7, § 7.2.8(D))	Failure to provide proportional services to nonpaying and low-income reimbursed patients in any year following licensure may result in the Department of Health's imposi-tion of one or more of the following penalties: 1. an approved plan of correction that remedies the failure through the additionalprovision of services in subsequent years, 2. a civil monetary penalty not to exceed $500,000, 3. suspension or revocation of the hospital's license, and 4. referral to CMS for sanctions under the Medicare and Medicaid programs. (N.M. Admin. Code tit. 7, § 7.2.8(L))

(Continued)

Rhode Island	As conditions of initial and continued licensure, all licensed hospitals shall 1. meet the statewide community standard for the provision of charity care; 2. meet standards for uncompensated care; 3. meet the statewide standards for the provision of community benefits. 4 not discourage persons who cannot afford to pay from seeking medical services; 5. not encourage persons who cannot afford to pay to seek essential medical services from other providers; 6. must annually report on compliance with these conditions, including (1) cost of charity care, (2) bad debt, (3) contract Medicaid shortfalls, and (4) any additional information demon-strating compliance with this section; and	• Charity care. • Uncompensated care. • Bad debt. • Medicaid shortfall. • Programs, procedures, and protocols that meet the needs of the medically indigent. • Linkages with community partners that focus on improving the health and well-being of community residents. • Non-revenue-producing services made available to the community, such as fitness programs, health screenings, or transportation services. • Public advocacy on behalf of community needs.	If any person knowingly violates or fails to comply or willingly or knowingly gives false or incorrect information the Directorof the Department of Health may, after notice and opportunityfor a prompt and fair hearing, deny, suspend, or revoke a license, or may order the licensee to admit or provide health services to no additional persons to the facility or to take corrective action necessary to secure compliance under the act; or the Superior Court may, after notice and opportunity for a prompt and fair hearing, impose a fine of not more than $1,000,000 or impose a prison term of not more than 5 years. (R.I. Gen. Laws § 23-17.14-30) If the Department of Health receives sufficient information indicating that a licensed hospital
	7. must have a formal, Board-approved plan for the provision of community benefits. The plan shall be updated and Board-approved at least every 3 years. (R.I. Gen. Laws §§ 23-17-43, 23-17.14-15; R.I. Code R. 14 090 007, 14 090 028)	• Scientific or medical research, or educational activities. • (R.I. Gen. Laws §§ 23-17-43, 23-17.14-15; R.I. Code R. 14 090 007, 14 090 028)	is not in compliance withthis section, the Director of the Department of Health shall hold a hearing upon 10 days notice tothe licensed hospital and shall issue in writing findings and appropriate penalties. (R.I. Gen. Laws § 23-17.14-15)

Source: GAO analysis of Massachusetts, New Mexico, and Rhode Island statutes and regulations.

Note: Although these states have community benefit provisions tied to licensure requirements, we did not include them in our list of states with community benefit requirements because their community benefit provisions are not tied to tax exemption or nonprofit status.

APPENDIX VI: EXAMPLES OF STATES WITH ONLY COMMUNITY BENEFIT REPORTING PROVISIONS

State	Description of requirements	Activities included in the definition of community benefit	Penalties
Connecticut	Biennial report on whether the hospital has in place a community benefits program. If the hospital has chosen to have a community benefits program, the report shall include a number of specified elements. (Conn. Gen. Stat. Ann. § 19a-27k)	• Preventive care. • Programs that improve the health status for working families and populations at risk in the community. (Conn. Gen. Stat. Ann. § 19a-127k)	The Commissioner of Public Health may, after notice and opportunity for a hearing, impose a civil penalty on any hospital that fails to submit the required report by the specifieddate. Such penalty shall be not more than $50 a day for each day after the required submittaldate that such report is not submitted. (Conn. Gen. Stat. Ann. § 19a-127k(f))
Georgia	Nonprofit hospitals must file an annual community benefit report disclosing the cost of indigent and charity care provided during the preceding year not later than 90 days after the close of the fiscal or calendar year. The report shall include a statement of the cost and type of indigent	• Indigent care. • Charity care. (Ga. Code Ann. § 31-7-90.1)	None specified.

(Continued)

	and charity care provided by the authority, including the number of indigent persons served, categorization of those persons by county of residence, as well as the cost of indigent and charity care provided by the authority, including the number of indigent persons served, categorization of those persons by county of residence, as well as the cost of indigent and charity care provided in dollars. (Ga. Code Ann. §§ 14-3-305; 31-7-90.1)		
Minnesota	Annual report of services provided to benefit the community. (Minn. Stat. §§ 144.698, 144.699)	• Services provided at no cost or for a reduced fee to patients unable to pay. • Teaching and research activities. • Community care. • Underpayment for services provided under state health care programs. • Research. • Community health services. • Financial and in-kind contributions. • Community building activities. • Community benefit operations. • Education. • Subsidized services. Does not include bad debt and underpayment for Medicare services. (Minn. Stat. Ann. §§ 144.698, 144.699)	None specified.

Nevada	Each hospital with at least 100 beds must file as required by the Director of the Department of Health and Human Services but at least annually the	• Goods, services, and resources provided by a hospital to a community to address the specific needs and concerns of that community. • Services provided by a hospital to uninsured and	None specified.
	expenses incurred for providing community benefits, a statement of its policies and procedures for providing discounted services to persons without health insurance, and a statement of its policies regarding collection. (Nev. Rev. Stat. § 449.490)	underserved persons. • Training programs for employees. • Health care services provided in areas that have a critical shortage of such services. (Nev. Rev. Stat. § 449.490)	
Oregon	Within 90 days of filing a Medicare cost report, a hospital must submit a community benefit report to the Office for Oregon Health Policy and Research of the community benefits provided by the hospital. (2007 Or. Laws 3290 (effective Jan. 1, 2008))	• Charity care. • Losses related to Medicaid, Medicare, State Children's Health Insurance Program, or other publicly funded health care program shortfalls. • Community health improvement services. • Research. • Financial and in-kind contributions to the community. • Community-building activities affecting health in the community. (2007 Or. Laws 3290 (effective Jan. 1, 2008))	Any health care facility that fails to comply may be subject to a civil penalty, not to exceed $500 per day of violation, determined by the severity of the violation. Civil penalties may be remitted or mitigated upon such terms and conditionsas the Administrator of the Office for Oregon Health Policy and Research considers proper and consistent with the public health and safety. (2007 Or. Laws 3290 (effective Jan. 1, 2008))

Source: GAO analysis of Connecticut, Georgia, Minnesota, Nevada, and Oregon statutes and regulations.

Notes: We did not consider these states to have community benefit requirements because their community benefit provisions do not require the provision of any community benefits. Connecticut's community benefit provisions are voluntary. Georgia, Minnesota, Nevada, and Oregon's community benefit provisions only require that hospitals report their community benefits without explicitly requiring the provision of community benefits.

Appendix VII: Examples of States with Community Benefit Provisions Located Outside of Statutes and Regulations

State	Description of requirements	Activities included in the definition of community benefit	Penalties
Massachusetts	Voluntary. (The Attorney General's Community Benefits Guidelines for Non-Profit Acute Care Hospitals at 1)	• Community health education. • Free preventive care or health screening services. • Mobile health vans. • Home care consistent with the definition of net charity care. • Medical and clinical education and research. • Support for and participation in community-oriented training programs. • Low- or negative-margin services offered in response to an identified community need. • Violence-reduction education and counseling. • Anti-smoking education. • Substance abuse education, prevention, and treatment. • Domestic violence reduction education and training. • Early childhood wellness programs. • Expanded prescription drug programs. • Volunteer services. • Net financial assistance to community health centers. • Unfunded services ancillary to Medicaid or Medicare services. (The Attorney General's Community Benefits Guidelines for Non-Profit Acute Care Hospitals at 10–11)	None specified (program is voluntary).
Utah	"Gift to the community" standard for property tax exemption: the hospital must establish that its total gift to the community exceeds on an annual basis its property tax liability for that year. (Property Tax Exemptions Standards of Practice at 2-35)	• Indigent care. • Community education and service, including research and professional education. • Medical discounts, including unreimbursed care covered by Medicare, Medicaid, or other similar government entitlement programs. • Donations of time. • Donations of money. (Property Tax Exemptions Standards of Practice at 2-35–2-36)	None specified.

Source: GAO analysis of the Massachusetts Attorney General's Community Benefit Guidelines for Non-Profit Acute Care Hospitals and Utah's Property Tax Exemptions Standards of Practice.

Note: Although these states have community benefit provisions outside of codified statutes and regulations, we did not include them in our list of states with community benefit requirements.

End Notes

[1] For purposes of this chapter, nonprofit hospitals refer to nongovernmental, acute care, general hospitals organized and operated for a charitable purpose and not designed primarily for profit-making purposes. Nonprofit hospitals qualify for tax-exempt status if they meet the requirements of section 501(c)(3) of the Internal Revenue Code.

[2] These requirements include restrictions on the entity's organizational and operational structure, and political activities.

[3] *See* H.R. Rep. No. 1860, 75th Cong., 3d Sess., 19 (1938).

[4] JCT estimated the following values of exemptions for nonprofit hospitals and their supporting organizations in 2002: $2.5 billion in federal income tax, $1.8 billion in federal bond financing, $1.8 billion in federal charitable contributions, $500 million in state corporate income tax, $2.8 billion in state and local sales taxes, and $3.1 billion in local property tax. See Congressional Budget Office, *Nonprofit Hospitals and Tax Arbitrage* (Washington, D.C.: December 2006).

[5] Charity care is generally defined as care provided to patients whom the hospital deems unable to pay all or a portion of their bills.

[6] U.S. Census Bureau, *Income, Poverty, and Health Insurance Coverage in the United States: 2006* (Washington, D.C., 2007). See also GAO, *21st Century Challenges: Reexamining the Base of the Federal Government*, GAO-05-325SP (Washington, D.C.: Feb. 1, 2005), in which ensuring that all Americans have access to a defined minimum core of essential health services and allocating responsibility for financing such services are identified as major health care challenges for the 21st century.

[7] The Emergency Medical Treatment and Active Labor Act applies to hospitals participating in Medicare. See 42 U.S.C. § 1395dd (2000). According to federal regulations, a hospital that provides emergency services must medically screen all persons who come to the hospital seeking emergency care to determine whether an emergency medical condition exists. If the hospital determines that a person has an emergency medical condition, the hospital must provide treatment necessary to stabilize that person or arrange for an appropriate transfer to another facility. See 42 C.F.R. § 489.24 (2007).

[8] Institute of Medicine, *Hidden Costs, Values Lost: Uninsurance in America* (Washington, D.C.: National Academies Press, 2003).

[9] Hospitals may not absorb all the costs associated with caring for the uninsured because they receive direct payments from different government sources to help cover their unreimbursed costs, including those for charity care, bad debt, and low-income patients. For example, Medicare and Medicaid make payments to hospitals that serve a disproportionate share of low-income patients under their respective disproportionate share hospital programs. Other state payments may also be available to hospitals, although their specific types vary widely. For example, hospitals may receive payments from special revenues, such as tobacco settlement funds; uncompensated care pools that are funded by provider contributions; and payment programs targeted at certain services, such as emergency services.

[10] Bad debt is generally defined as the uncollectible payment that the patient is expected to, but does not, pay.

[11] For this study, we analyzed 2003 data from five geographically diverse states—California, Florida, Georgia, Indiana, and Texas—with substantial representation of the three ownership groups. For each state, we determined the three ownership groups' percentages of total uncompensated care costs and patient operating expenses devoted to uncompensated care. See GAO, *Nonprofit, For-Profit, and Government Hospitals: Uncompensated Care and Other Community Benefits*, GAO-05-743T (Washington, D.C.: May 26, 2005).

[12] CBO found that, on average, nonprofit hospitals provided more uncompensated care than otherwise similar for-profit hospitals, although the ranges of uncompensated care provided by the two types of hospitals largely overlapped. See Congressional Budget Office,

Nonprofit Hospitals and the Provision of Community Benefits (Washington, D.C.: December 2006).

[13] U.S. Senate, Committee on Finance, minority staff, *Tax-Exempt Hospitals: Discussion Draft*, July 19, 2007.

[14] For purposes of this chapter, unless otherwise apparent, "states" refers to the 50 states and the District of Columbia.

[15] For the remainder of this chapter, we will refer to VHA Inc., formerly known as Voluntary Hospitals of America, as VHA.

[16] Medicare, financed by the federal government, provides health care coverage to eligible individuals aged 65 years or older, certain individuals with disabilities, and individuals with end-stage renal disease.

[17] While CMS is not responsible for administering U.S. tax law, the agency was directed by Congress to collect data on costs incurred by hospitals for providing services for which the hospitals are not compensated. Many of these services and their associated costs are defined as community benefit by both IRS and industry groups.

[18] For purposes of this chapter, we refer to CHA and VHA in tandem because they jointly issued the guidance.

[19] For purposes of this chapter, we refer to the nonprofit health systems, hospital systems, and health care systems we interviewed as "health care systems."

[20] Reliable, hospital-specific, nationwide data were not available.

[21] The unreimbursed costs of government health care programs—commonly referred to by industry groups as "shortfalls"—are generally defined as the difference created when a facility receives payments that are less than the facility's costs of caring for public program beneficiaries.

[22] Medicaid provides health care coverage to eligible low-income people, and is jointly financed by the federal government and the states.

[23] Percentage total is greater than 100 due to rounding.

[24] See, e.g., Geisinger Health Plan v. Comm'r, 985 F.2d 1210, 1216 (3rd Cir. 1993) (discussing IRS policy and cases construing exemption provisions for hospitals).

[25] Harding Hospital, Inc. v. U.S., 505 F.2d 1068, 1071-72 (6th Cir. 1974).

[26] Revenue rulings are published IRS administrative decisions stating how the agency applies provisions of tax law to a particular set of circumstances.

[27] Rev. Rul. 56-185, 1956-1 C.B. 202.

[28] Rev. Rul. 69-545, 1969-2 C.B. 117.

[29] Specifically, the 1969 revenue ruling removed the 1956 revenue ruling requirement relating to caring for patients without charge or at rates below cost, and indicated that hospitals could qualify for federal tax exemption if they provided a benefit to the community.

[30] In a 1983 revenue ruling, IRS provided that at least in the case where a state health planning agency made an independent determination that operation of an emergency room would be unnecessary and duplicative, a hospital could still qualify for tax exemption even though it did not operate an emergency room. Rev. Rul. 83-157, 1983-2 C.B. 94.

[31] All qualified physicians who meet the hospital's guidelines can be part of the hospital staff.

[32] Starting in tax year 2008, exempt organizations with gross receipts less than $25,000 will need to file Form 990-N. Those with gross receipts less than $1,000,000 (to be reduced to $200,000 by tax year 2010) and total assets less than $2,500,000 (to be reduced to $500,000 by tax year 2010) will file Form 990-EZ, instead of the full Form 990. Forms 990-N and 990-EZ are shorter than the full Form 990.

[33] We examined IRS's final version of the Form 990, which was pending the Office of Management and Budget's approval at the time this chapter was issued. Form 990's new Schedule H requires nonprofit hospitals to report their provision of bad debt, the unreimbursed cost of Medicare, and community-building activities in Parts II and III of the schedule, but not as part of the Part I quantifiable community benefit table. Prior to this revision, Form 990 did not collect and IRS did not have information on hospitals' provision

of activities that benefit the community in specified categories. IRS officials indicated that for tax years 2001 to 2006, none of the nonprofit hospital examinations the agency conducted were selected specifically to ascertain whether these hospitals complied with the community benefit standard. Rather, IRS conducted these examinations in the course of the agency's other work. These officials also told us that some of these examinations were full-scale examinations where in addition to reviewing other issues, IRS conducted a limited review of community benefit focusing on the five factors listed in the 1969 revenue ruling.

[34] While Part V, Facility Information, of Schedule H is required for tax year 2008, Parts I, II, III, IV, and VI do not become mandatory until tax year 2009. Depending on when a hospital's fiscal year begins, tax year 2009 can start on any date during calendar year 2009 and end 12 months later, which could be as late as November 30, 2010. IRS officials have noted that hospitals have until 5 months after the end of their fiscal year to file Form 990 and its schedules. Beyond this filing deadline, hospitals may also obtain filing extensions for an additional 6 months.

[35] Medicare-certified institutional providers are required to submit an annual cost report. The cost report contains provider information, such as facility characteristics, as well as utilization, cost, charge, and financial statement data. For cost report periods beginning on or after October 1, 2001, section 112(b) of the Medicare, Medicaid, and SCHIP Balanced Budget Refinement Act of 1999 (BBRA) requires short stay, acute care hospitals to submit cost reports containing data on costs incurred by the hospital for providing inpatient and outpatient hospital services for which the hospital is not compensated, including non-Medicare bad debt, charity care, and charges for Medicaid and indigent care. Pub. L.No. 106-113, App. F., § 112(b), 113 Stat. 1501, 1501A-330.

[36] The State Children's Health Insurance Program provides health care coverage to uninsured children in families whose incomes exceed the eligibility requirements of Medicaid. States have some flexibility in how they design their programs.

[37] MedPAC was established by the Balanced Budget Act of 1997, § 4022, 42 U.S.C. § 1395b-6 (2000), to advise Congress on issues affecting the Medicare program.

[38] See Geisinger Health Plan v. Comm'r, 985 F.2d 1210, 1217 (3d Cir. 1993) ("[N]o clear test has emerged to apply to nonprofit hospitals seeking tax exemptions.").

[39] The five factors were (1) the operation of an emergency room open to all members of the community without regard to ability to pay; (2) a governance board composed of independent civic leaders; (3) the use of surplus revenue for facilities improvement, patient care, and medical training, education, and research; (4) the provision of inpatient hospital care for all persons in the community able to pay, including those covered by Medicare and Medicaid; and (5) an open medical staff with privileges available to all qualifying physicians.

[40] Statement of Mark Everson, Commissioner of Internal Revenue, testimony before the full House Committee on Ways and Means, May 26, 2005.

[41] Harding Hosp. Inc. v. United States, 505 F. 2d 1068, 1077 (6th Cir. 1974).

[42] IHC Health Plans, Inc. v. Comm'r, 325 F.3d 1188, 1197 n.16 (10th Cir. 2003) (citing Geisinger Health Plan v. Comm'r, 985 F.2d 1210, 1218 (3d Cir. 1993); Fed'n Pharmacy Serv., Inc. v. Comm'r, 625 F.2d 804, 807 (8th Cir. 1980); and Sound Health Ass'n v. Comm'r, 71 T.C. 158, 1978 WL 3393 (1978)).

[43] IHC Health Plans, Inc., 325 F.3d at 1197–98.

[44] Some of the 36 states that do not have community benefit requirements have provisions or other resources related to community benefit. Some states, including Massachusetts, New Mexico, and Rhode Island, have community benefit provisions tied to their hospital licensure requirements rather than requirements needed to obtain and maintain tax-exempt or nonprofit status. At least five states—Connecticut, Georgia, Minnesota, Nevada, and Oregon—require that hospitals periodically report to the relevant authorities the community benefits they provide but do not require that hospitals actually provide any community benefits. At least two states—Massachusetts and Utah—describe their community benefit

provisions in sources other than statutes or regulations, such as attorney general guidelines or property tax exemption standards. We provide examples of states that fall into these categories as anecdotal evidence; they do not represent a comprehensive analysis of states without community benefit requirements as we define that term.

[45] For state requirements tied to tax-exempt or nonprofit status, a hospital can be assessed a civil penalty if it fails to comply with state community benefit requirements. Hospitals in such states may also be denied tax exemption, although we did not consider that to be a penalty for purposes of this chapter. If a state has no community benefit requirement but ties community benefit provisions to licensure, such as Massachusetts, New Mexico, and Rhode Island, a hospital in that state may be denied licensure for failure to comply with state community benefit provisions (or if already licensed, its license can be suspended or revoked). Some state requirements do not provide any penalty for failure to comply.

[46] The 10 states with detailed requirements are California, Idaho, Illinois, Indiana, Maryland, New Hampshire, New York, Pennsylvania, Texas, and West Virginia.

[47] The five states with less-detailed requirements are Alabama, Colorado, Mississippi, North Dakota, and Wyoming.

[48] Cal. Health & Safety Code §§ 127350, 127355 (2008).

[49] 210 Ill. Comp. Stat. 76/15, 76/20 (2008).

[50] Illinois defines community benefit to include the unreimbursed cost of providing charity care, language assistant services, government-sponsored indigent health care, donations, volunteer services, education, government-sponsored program services, research, subsidized health services, and collecting bad debts. Illinois' definition explicitly excludes the cost of paying taxes or other governmental assessments. Maryland defines community benefit as an activity that is intended to address community needs and priorities primarily through disease prevention and improvement of health status, including health services provided to vulnerable or underserved populations, such as Medicaid, Medicare, or Maryland Children's Health Program enrollees; financial or in-kind support of public health programs; donations of funds, property, or other resources that contribute to a community priority; health care cost containment activities; and health education, screening, and prevention services.

[51] CMS added this chaptering instrument pursuant to section 112(b) of the BBRA, which does not use the term "community benefit," but requires short stay, acute care hospitals to submit data on costs incurred by the hospital for providing services for which the hospital is not compensated, including non-Medicare bad debt, charity care, and charges for Medicaid and indigent care.

[52] Making such charity care determinations is based in large part on information supplied by the patient or on the patient's behalf in the form of documentation, such as federal tax returns, pay stubs, bank statements, etc. There are many reasons that hospitals may be unable to obtain the necessary documentation. For example, a hospital association official we spoke with stated that hospitals are required to treat and stabilize emergency patients before inquiring about the patients' need for charity care, but patients may leave the hospital before hospital officials can speak to them about financial assistance. Other reasons include patient embarrassment or a lack of understanding of the hospital's charity care policy.

[53] Specifically, HFMA stated that hospitals may refer to external sources, such as credit reports, to help support charity care determinations. Some of the hospital and hospital association officials we spoke with are either using or exploring the possibility of using external sources, such as zip codes in conjunction with per-capita income data, credit reports, and migrant worker status, as proxies to make charity care eligibility determinations in the absence of patient-provided documentation. HFMA further stated that providers should make every effort to determine charity care eligibility before or at the time of service, but such determinations can also be made during a specific time period following patient care.

[54] We did not reduce bad debt expenses to costs because we found that hospitals did not consistently report bad debt in costs or charges.

[55] CMS has stated that Medicare payments to hospitals under the prospective payment system cover the costs of an efficient provider.

[56] HFMA states that hospitals that choose to define the unreimbursed cost of Medicare as community benefit should disclose that cost separately from charity care, accompanied by detail and context to help readers understand the reported cost.

[57] Texas considers the unreimbursed cost of non-means-tested government health care programs, including Medicare, as community benefit.

[58] Cash and in-kind contributions to others include cash donations, grants, and in-kind donations made to individuals or the community at large.

[59] Community benefit operations include dedicated staff, community health needs assessments, and other resources.

[60] Community health improvement services include programs for community health education, community-based clinical services, and health care support services.

[61] Health professions education includes education for physicians, medical students, nurses, nursing students, and other health professionals, and scholarships and funding for professional education.

[62] Medical research includes both clinical and community health research.

[63] Subsidized health services are clinical services provided at a financial loss and subsidized by the hospital; common examples include emergency and trauma services, and burn units.

[64] Community-building activities include physical improvements and housing programs, economic development, community support, environmental improvements, leadership development and leadership training for community members, coalition building, community health improvement advocacy, and workforce development.

[65] Although there is consensus to include community benefit operations as community benefit, data are also not available to evaluate the cost associated with this activity compared to other community benefits.

[66] An EIN is an identification number used by IRS in the administration of tax laws.

[67] Medicare Payment Advisory Commission, *Report to the Congress: Medicare Payment Policy* (Washington, D.C., 2007).

[68] MedPAC has been consulting with CMS to revise Worksheet S-10 and the accompanying instructions.

[69] A cost-accounting system is a continuous and systematic process designed to accumulate and assign costs routinely or as desired by management.

[70] CCRs are ratios applied to charges in order to estimate costs, which are used in Medicare.

[71] Uncompensated care pools are a financing mechanism to redistribute, within a state, hospitals' financial burdens of caring for patients who do not have the ability to pay. Uncompensated care programs can include, for example, programs outside the hospital that provide health care services to financially indigent patients.

[72] HFMA specifies that while hospitals should not subtract payments from uncompensated care pools from charity care costs, these payments should be separately disclosed if they are of sufficient size. HFMA does not specify how hospitals should treat their contributions to uncompensated care pools.

[73] California, Indiana, and Texas state data did not have data on both contributions to and payments from uncompensated pools or programs. The uncompensated care pool in Massachusetts is primarily funded by an assessment on hospitals, a surcharge on insurers, and an annual appropriation from the general fund.

[74] DSH payments are meant to compensate those hospitals that care for a disproportionate number of low-income patients.

[75] The percentages remain the same because only four nonprofit hospitals reported Medicaid DSH payments in the Massachusetts state data and the amount these hospitals reported was small in comparison to the amount of unreimbursed cost of Medicaid.

[76] States may receive federal matching funds for provider taxes only if such fees are broad- based (that is, imposed on all items or services in the class of services or providers thereof);

uniformly imposed (that is, all items or services in the class or providers thereof pay the same rate of tax); and do not result in any taxpayers being held harmless (that is, receiving state funds to reduce the net payment to the state to below the amount of the tax). 42 U.S.C. § 1396b(w)(3), (6) (2000).

[77] These five factors are (1) the operation of an emergency room open to all members of the community without regard to ability to pay; (2) a governance board composed of community members; (3) the use of surplus revenue for facilities improvement, patient care, and medical training, education, and research; (4) the provision of inpatient hospital care for all persons in the community able to pay, including those covered by Medicare and Medicaid; and (5) an open medical staff with privileges available to all qualifying physicians.

[78] Reliable, hospital-specific, nationwide data were not available.

[79] For purposes of this chapter, we refer to the nonprofit health systems, hospital systems, and health care systems we interviewed as "health care system."

[80] Examples of provisions that we excluded using this criterion include vaccination mandates and newborn screening requirements.

[81] 42 U.S.C. § 1395dd (2000).

[82] Conn. Gen. Stat. Ann. § 19a-127k(a), (c) (West 2008).

[83] Conn. Gen. Stat. Ann. § 19a-127k(b) (West 2008).

[84] Ga. Code Ann. § 14-3-305(d) (2008).

[85] Minn. Stat. Ann. § 144.698, .699 (West 2008).

[86] Nev. Rev. Stat. 449.490(3)(b) (2008).

[87] 2007 Or. Laws 3290.

[88] This position is shared by Community Catalyst in developing its compendium of state community benefit requirements. See Community Catalyst, *Health Care Community Benefits: A Compendium of State Laws* (Boston, 2007).

[89] Idaho Code § 63-602D(4) (Michie 2008).

[90] Idaho Code § 63-602D(7) (Michie 2008).

[91] Ariz. Rev. Stat. § 43-1201 (2008).

[92] We examined IRS's final version of the Form 990, which was pending the Office of Management and Budget's approval at the time this chapter was issued.

[93] Medicaid provides health care coverage to eligible low-income people, and is jointly financed by the federal government and the states.

[94] We defined "community benefit requirement" as a legal standard that expressly obligates a hospital to provide health care services or benefits to the community served by the hospital as a condition of maintaining tax-exempt status or qualifying as a nonprofit hospital. It is generally something that hospitals are required to do beyond their role of providing care for the sick and injured in exchange for remuneration or compensation. We considered the requirement to be one applicable to hospitals only if it either expressly referred to hospitals or expressly referred to care or services of the nature and type that one would reasonably expect to be provided by or performed primarily at acute care hospitals.

[95] For purposes of this chapter, unless otherwise apparent, "states" refers to the 50 states and the District of Columbia.

[96] The 10 states with detailed community benefit requirements are California, Idaho, Illinois, Indiana, Maryland, New Hampshire, New York, Pennsylvania, Texas, and West Virginia.

[97] 210 Ill. Comp. Stat. 76/10 (2008).

[98] Md. Code Ann., Health–Gen. § 19-303(a)(3) (2008).

[99] Cal. Health & Safety Code § 127350 (West 2008).

[100] Those five states are Alabama, Colorado, Mississippi, North Dakota, and Wyoming. These states typically do not use the term "community benefit" or similar terms such as "community service" or "gift to the community," although they may refer to "charity care" or "charity patients." Rather, the language of their provisions approximates the concept of

community benefit, and so we consider them to have community benefit requirements. See our definition of "community benefit" in appendix I.

[101] Ala. Code § 40-9-1(2) (2008).

[102] Wyo. R. & Regs. Rev. Gen. Ch. 14 § 10(a) (2008).

[103] Examples of these states include Connecticut, Georgia, Minnesota, Nevada, and Oregon. Oregon is the most recent state to pass a community benefit law. Its law, passed in 2007, became effective on January 1, 2008. The law includes a detailed definition of community benefit, directs the Office for Oregon Health Policy and Research to adopt a cost-based community benefit reporting system for hospitals operating in Oregon that is consistent with established national standards for hospital reporting of community benefits, and sets forth civil penalties for health care facilities that fail to comply with the reporting system. 2007 Or. Laws 3290 (effective Jan. 1, 2008; to be added to Or. Rev. Stat. Ch. 442).

[104] *See* Property Tax Division, Utah State Tax Commission, Property Tax Exemptions Standards of Practice (2007).

[105] *See* Office of Attorney General, Commonwealth of Mass., The Attorney General's Community Benefits Guidelines for Non-Profit Acute Care Hospitals (2007).

[106] Some state codes and regulations provided penalties for failing to comply with community benefit requirements. We noted penalty provisions only if the penalty provision made a direct and express reference to failure to comply with the community benefit requirement as the basis for the penalty. We do not include statutory or regulatory references to denial of tax exemption for failure to comply as a penalty.

[107] Ind. Code 16-21-9-8 (2008); Md. Regs. Code tit. 10, § 37.01.03(N) (2008); and Tex. Health & Safety Code Ann. § 311.047 (Vernon 2008).

[108] N.M. Admin. Code tit. 7, § 7.2.8(L) (2008) and R.I. Gen. Laws § 23-17.14-30 (2008).

[109] R.I. Gen. Laws § 23-17.14-30 (2008).

[110] These states include Alabama, Mississippi, Pennsylvania, Texas, and West Virginia.

[111] Ala. Code § 40-9-1(2) (2008).

[112] Tex. Health & Safety Code Ann. § 311.045(b)(1) (Vernon 2008).

[113] Miss. Code Ann. § 27-31-1(f) (2008).

[114] W. Va. Code St. R. § 110-3-24.9.8 (2008).

[115] Cal. Health & Safety Code § 127350(d) (West 2008).

In: Nonprofit Hospitals and the Community... ISBN: 978-1-61761-999-1
Editor: Maria G. Reyes

Chapter 3

NONPROFIT HOSPITALS AND THE PROVISION OF COMMUNITY BENEFITS

Congressional Budget Office

INTRODUCTION AND SUMMARY

The various tax exemptions provided to nonprofit hospitals have come under scrutiny by policymakers, with the central concern being whether those hospitals provide community benefits that justify forgone government tax revenues. In this paper, the Congressional Budget Office (CBO) measures the provision of certain community benefits and compares nonprofit hospitals with for-profit hospitals. For-profit hospitals do not receive tax exemptions and are not required to meet community-benefit standards; the level of community benefits provided by for-profit hospitals serves, therefore, as a useful benchmark against which to compare nonprofit hospitals. The analysis also examines the provision of community benefits by nonfederal government hospitals.[1]

Although nonprofit hospitals must provide community benefits in order to receive tax exemptions, there is little consensus on what constitutes a community benefit or how to measure such benefits. For the purposes of this analysis, community benefits include the provision of uncompensated care, the provision of services to Medicaid patients, and the provision of certain specialized services that have been identified as generally unprofitable. Those services were selected because they benefit the community but are not typically considered financially rewarding.

In general, the comparisons of nonprofit and for-profit hospitals yielded mixed results. CBO found that, on average, nonprofit hospitals provided higher levels of uncompensated care than did otherwise similar for-profit hospitals. Among individual hospitals, however, the provision of uncompensated care varied widely, and the distributions for nonprofit and for-profit hospitals largely overlapped. Nonprofit hospitals were more likely than otherwise similar for-profit hospitals to provide certain specialized services but were found to provide care to fewer Medicaid-covered patients as a share of their total patient population. On average, nonprofit hospitals were found to operate in areas with higher average incomes, lower poverty rates, and lower rates of uninsurance than for-profit hospitals.

Provision of Uncompensated Care

The level of uncompensated care provided by community hospitals is examined here for hospitals located in five states—California, Florida, Georgia, Indiana, and Texas—using data from 2003 (the latest year for which such data are available).[2] "Uncompensated care" refers to the sum of charity care (services for which a hospital does not expect payment) and bad debt (services for which a hospital expects but does not collect payment). Although charity care is a better measure of the community benefits provided by a hospital, data limitations precluded CBO's analyzing charity care and bad debt separately.

The five selected states were chosen in part because sufficiently reliable data on uncompensated care were available in those areas. The data were provided to CBO by the Government Accountability Office (GAO) and were developed by GAO for use in its analyses of issues relating to the level of uncompensated care provided by different types of hospitals.[3] CBO's analysis expands on GAO's findings in several ways: first, regression techniques are used to calculate adjusted differences between nonprofit and for-profit hospitals in the provision of uncompensated care, taking into account hospital characteristics and the characteristics of local populations; and, second, the provision of Medicaid services and specialized services, such as emergency room care, are analyzed quantitatively.

CBO's five-state analysis of uncompensated care yielded the following key findings:

- In the five states analyzed, nonprofit hospitals provided a total of about $3 billion in uncompensated care, government hospitals provided more than $3 billion, and for-profit hospitals provided about $1 billion in uncompensated care. The difference in the total amount of uncompensated care provided by nonprofit and for-profit hospitals is largely attributable to the fact that nonprofit hospitals accounted for a much larger share of the hospital market than did for-profits.
- The average "uncompensated-care share"—the cost of uncompensated care as a share of hospitals' operating expenses—was much higher at government hospitals (13.0 percent) than at either nonprofit hospitals (4.7 percent) or for-profit hospitals (4.2 percent).
- Individual hospitals varied widely in their uncompensated-care shares. Although nonprofit hospitals, on average, have slightly higher uncompensated-care shares than for-profits (by 0.5 percentage points), the distributions of uncompensated-care shares among those two types of hospitals overlap to a large extent.
- When regression techniques were used to adjust for the hospitals' size and location and for the characteristics of the local populations, nonprofit hospitals were estimated to have an average uncompensated- care share that was 0.6 percentage points higher than that for otherwise similar for-profit hospitals. That estimated difference corresponds to nonprofit hospitals in the five selected states providing between $100 million and $700 million more in uncompensated care than would have been provided if they had been for-profits.[4]

Provision of Medicaid-Covered Services

Medicaid's payment rates have, in general, been found to be somewhat below the costs that hospitals incur in providing Medicaid-covered services. Because providing hospital services to Medicaid patients is often unprofitable and serves a needy population, it can be thought of as a type of community benefit. Among all community hospitals nationwide, CBO found that the Medicaid share—Medicaid-covered days as a share of all patient days—was, on average, 1.5 percentage points lower among nonprofit hospitals than it was among for-profit hospitals (15.6 percent versus 17.2 percent). The Medicaid share was substantially higher among government hospitals (27.0 percent). When regression techniques were used to control for hospital characteristics, nonprofit hospitals were found to have adjusted Medicaid shares that were 1.3 percentage points lower than those of otherwise similar for-profit hospitals.

Provision of Specialized Services

CBO also examined the share of hospitals of different ownership types that provide four specific types of specialized patient services: intensive care for burn victims, emergency room care, high-level trauma care, and labor and delivery services.[5] Each of those services addresses a community need and has been identified as being generally unprofitable. Among all community hospitals nationwide, emergency room care and labor and delivery services were both quite common, whereas few hospitals provided burn intensive care or high-level trauma care.

CBO found that nonprofit hospitals were more likely than for-profit hospitals to provide each of the four specialized services examined. After adjustment for hospital characteristics, nonprofit hospitals were found to be significantly more likely than for-profit hospitals to provide two of the four specialized patient services (emergency room care and labor and delivery services). Compared with otherwise similar for-profit hospitals, the share of nonprofit hospitals providing emergency room care was 3.8 percentage points higher, and the share providing labor and delivery services was 10.5 percentage points higher. CBO did not attempt to quantify the value to the community of the availability of those specialized services.

The Value of Tax Exemptions for Nonprofit Hospitals

The Joint Committee on Taxation (JCT) recently examined the value to nonprofit hospitals and their supporting organizations of the major tax exemptions they receive from federal, state, and local governments. Together, the value of the various tax exemptions in 2002 was estimated to be $12.6 billion, with exemptions from federal taxes accounting for about half of the total and exemptions from state and local taxes accounting for the remaining half.

JCT also estimated the value of some of the tax exemptions for nonprofit hospitals located in the five states for which uncompensated-care data were available. In those five states, the exemptions from federal and state corporate income taxes, state and local sales taxes, and local property taxes were valued at $2.5 billion. (Two important categories of tax exemptions—tax-exempt-bond financing and the deductibility of charitable contributions—were included in the national totals but were not available for the five states and are not included in the five-state total.)

BACKGROUND

The hospital industry in the United States includes a mix of ownership forms. Nonprofit hospitals are the most common type, but for-profit and government hospitals also play substantial roles.[6] Of the 630,000 beds in Medicare-certified community hospitals in the United States in 2003, 68 percent were located in nonprofit hospitals, 16 percent were located in for-profit hospitals, and 15 percent were located in government (nonfederal) facilities.

This section of the analysis examines the differences between nonprofit hospitals and for-profit hospitals in their ownership structure, tax treatment, and the provision of collective goods. (Collective goods are defined as goods or services that, when used or consumed, generate well-being or utility for more than one individual at the same time.[7]) The tax exemptions for nonprofit hospitals are discussed as one approach to promoting the provision of collective goods, and other approaches are identified as well.

Differences in Ownership Structure

Ownership of a business entity entails the right to direct the operations of that business and the right to receive its profits. Like for-profits, nonprofit hospitals have governing boards that guide their operations. And, like for-profits, nonprofit hospitals may earn surpluses or accounting profits, meaning an excess of revenues over expenses. But nonprofits face a "nondistribution constraint," which means that they do not have shareholders and may not distribute surpluses to managers, individual owners, or members of the governing board. Surpluses generated by nonprofit hospitals' activities are expected to be reinvested in the hospitals' operations rather than distributed to individual owners.

Differences in Tax Treatment

Nonprofit hospitals receive tax exemptions that allow them to use funds that would have been paid in taxes for patient care or other purposes. Tax exemptions provided to nonprofit hospitals, therefore, can be viewed as a form of government subsidy for the activities of a certain type of hospital. Whether that subsidy is justified from a public policy perspective depends on whether policymakers believe that the activities of hospitals in general should be subsidized, and, if so, whether those subsidies should be targeted at hospitals that organize themselves as nonprofits.

One possible rationale for providing tax exemptions to nonprofit hospitals would be if nonprofit hospitals tended to provide more collective goods than did for- profit hospitals. The provision of uncompensated medical care to an indigent individual might be thought of as a type of collective good: the medical care directly benefits the indigent individual who receives it and might also benefit members of the community (by fulfilling compassionate impulses, for example, or by preventing the spread of a communicable disease). The managers of nonprofit organizations, because they do not directly receive the profits from the activities they oversee, might, in principle, be more willing than the managers of for-profit firms to provide collective goods when doing so is unprofitable.[8]

Unlike for-profit hospitals, nonprofit hospitals are generally exempt from federal and state corporate income taxes, and local sales and property taxes. Nonprofit hospitals can also obtain tax-exempt-bond financing and receive charitable contributions that are tax-deductible to the donor. For a hospital to qualify for exemption from federal income taxes, it must be organized and operated exclusively for a charitable, educational, or scientific purpose and meet Internal Revenue Service (IRS) requirements under section 501(c) (3) of the tax code.

The IRS does not specifically require that a hospital provide a certain level of charity care to qualify for tax- exempt status, as long as the hospital provides some benefits to the community. The criteria the IRS uses to determine whether a hospital qualifies as tax-exempt have changed over time and have been the subject of some debate. Activities that could support a hospital's application for federal tax-exempt status include operating an emergency room that is open to all members of the community regardless of their ability to pay; having a governing board composed of community members; and using earnings to improve facilities, patient care, medical education, training, and research.

To qualify for exemption from state corporate income taxes and for exemption from state and local property and sales taxes, hospitals are subject to local requirements that may differ from federal requirements. State and local governments have, in many cases, required that, in order to receive tax exemptions, hospitals meet standards that are stricter than those imposed by the IRS. For example, in 1985 the Utah Supreme Court ruled that, to qualify for the property-tax exemption, hospitals must engage in some "act of giving," such as providing charity care. In Illinois, property-tax exemptions are limited to nonprofit hospitals that dispense charity care to all who need it. Some states have already taken or have proposed taking the additional step of imposing specific reporting and performance requirements on nonprofit hospitals. For example, in Texas, to receive a property-tax exemption, nonprofit hospitals must regularly report on the charity care and other community benefits that they provide and must meet specified quantitative standards.[9] Those state and local requirements can represent significant constraints on nonprofit hospitals, given the financial value to nonprofit hospitals of the exemptions from state and local taxes.

To evaluate how nonprofit hospitals currently meet the community benefits standard, the IRS recently distributed a questionnaire to a selected group of nonprofit hospitals. Those hospitals were asked to provide a detailed report on their community-benefit policies, admissions policies, billing policies, and the amount of uncompensated care they provide. The IRS may use the responses to the questionnaire to issue further guidance or standards relating to tax exemptions for nonprofit hospitals.

The Value of Tax Exemptions for Nonprofit Hospitals

JCT recently examined the value to nonprofit hospitals of the major tax exemptions they receive from federal, state, and local governments.[10] Together, the value of the various tax exemptions for nonprofit hospitals nationwide was estimated to be $12.6 billion in 2002 (see Table 1). Exemptions from federal taxes accounted for about half of the total, and state and local taxes accounted for the other half. The largest categories were the exemption from local property taxes ($3.1 billion) and the exemption from state and local sales taxes ($2.8 billion). (The exemption from sales taxes applies to supplies that nonprofit hospitals purchase, such as medical and office equipment.)

JCT also estimated the value of certain tax exemptions provided to nonprofit hospitals located in the five states for which GAO data on uncompensated care were available. In those five states, the exemptions from the federal and state corporate income taxes, state and local sales taxes, and local property taxes in 2002 were valued at $2.5 billion. (Two important categories of tax exemptions—tax-exempt-bond financing and the deductibility of charitable contributions—were included in the national totals but were not calculated for the five states and are not included in the five-state total.)

In terms of reduced tax revenues, the costs to the various levels of government of the tax exemptions for nonprofit hospitals are difficult to quantify. Part of the difficulty in measuring the value of the tax exemptions arises from the fact that nonprofits, because of their tax-exempt status, do not file the same types of tax returns as for-profits and, thus, do not provide some information needed to calculate their potential tax liability. A more fundamental issue in valuing the tax exemptions provided to nonprofits is the fact that nonprofit hospitals, if they were to lose their tax-exempt status, would likely change their behavior.

To calculate the value of the tax exemptions listed in Table 1, hospitals' observed tax bases were multiplied by the applicable tax rates. That method follows JCT's standard approach to calculating "tax expenditures," which are defined as revenue losses resulting from special provisions or preferences in tax law.[11] The calculation of tax expenditures implicitly assumes no behavioral responses—in other words, it assumes that if special tax preferences were removed there would be no change in firms' income, capital structure, or physical assets. A revenue estimate, which is the estimated change in tax revenues arising from a change in tax policy, differs from a tax expenditure in that the revenue estimate incorporates behavioral responses. The value of the tax exemptions detailed in Table 1 does not incorporate behavioral responses and should not be interpreted as revenue estimates.

Identifying the potential behavioral responses of non-profit hospitals to removal of or restrictions on tax exemptions is complex. If nonprofit hospitals lost their tax-exempt status but maintained their nonprofit ownership status, they would face financial pressure to reduce their accounting profits and thereby reduce their tax burden.[12] That pressure could lead nonprofit hospitals to change their accounting practices as well as lower the prices they charge patients and insurers, and increase their costs of production.[13] At the same time, adding new restrictions on tax-exempt status for nonprofit hospitals might prompt some of those facilities to convert to for- profit ownership, which might also result in changes in their tax bases (taxable income for converting hospitals, for example, might increase).

Table 1. Estimated Value of Tax Exemptions Provided to Nonprofit Hospitals, 2002

	Value (Billions of dollars)
Corporate Income Tax (Federal)	2.5
Tax-Exempt-Bond Financing (Federal)	1.8
Charitable Contributions (Federal)	1.8
Corporate Income Tax (State)	0.5
Sales Tax (State and local)	2.8
Property Tax (Local)	3.1
Total	**12.6**

Source: Joint Committee on Taxation.

Approaches to Providing Collective Goods

Besides offering tax exemptions to nonprofit hospitals, governments have several options if they wish to promote the provision of collective goods such as health care for low-income individuals. The first approach is to produce those goods directly. Government hospitals that provide charity care are an example of direct production. The second approach is to purchase collective goods from private organizations. An example of that approach is the Medicaid program, through which the federal government and state governments purchase health care from private organizations on behalf of low-income individuals. The third approach is to subsidize the activities of producers of collective goods. Subsidies have the advantage of flexibility—local organizations can direct the use of the subsidies to meet locally identified needs—but potentially have the disadvantage of being poorly targeted.

Unlike the tax exemptions provided to nonprofit hospitals, other subsidy mechanisms exist that are available to hospitals of all ownership types. Such subsidies include Medicare and Medicaid disproportionate share hospital (DSH) payments and Medicare's supplemental payments to teaching hospitals through the indirect medical education (IME) program.[14] Hospitals may also receive partial reimbursement from Medicare for bad debt incurred for Medicare patients.[15] In addition, some states fund hospitals through various revenue sources such as tobacco- settlement funds and uncompensated-care pools.

The existing subsidies for hospital care, other than the tax exemptions provided to nonprofits, are substantial. CBO estimates that in 2005 hospitals received $15 billion in Medicare DSH and IME payments, and $9 billion in Medicaid DSH payments.[16] Other analysts have estimated that Medicare bad-debt payments to hospitals totaled $1.6 billion in 2005, and that in 2001 state and local governments provided about $7 billion to hospitals through various tax appropriations and indigent-care programs.[17]

DEFINING COMMUNITY BENEFITS

Although nonprofit hospitals receive tax exemptions in return for providing community benefits, there is little consensus on what constitutes a community benefit or how to measure community benefits. In the academic literature, community benefits have been defined as "those programs and services that are generally thought to be provided at low or negative margin and are intended to improve access by disadvantaged groups or to address important health care matters for a defined population."[18] Community benefits and collective goods are linked—if a hospital chooses to provide a particular medical service despite its being unprofitable, that may indicate that the hospital views that service as a collective good that is worth providing because it benefits the community. In identifying and measuring the community benefits that hospitals provide, it seems reasonable, therefore, to focus on services that are uncompensated or relatively unprofitable.

The IRS has developed a practical definition of community benefits for the purpose of granting tax exemptions. The federal criteria for providing tax exemptions to nonprofit hospitals have changed over time and have been gradually loosened. In a 1956 revenue ruling, the IRS criteria included a charity-care requirement, meaning specifically that a hospital "must be operated to the extent of its financial ability for those not able to pay for the services rendered."[19] That 1956 revenue ruling specified clearly that bad debt did not constitute charity and that incurring bad debt did not satisfy the criteria for the tax exemption. In a 1969 revenue ruling, the IRS significantly loosened the criteria for nonprofit hospitals to receive the federal income tax exemption and defined promoting the health of any broad class of persons as a community benefit, including, perhaps, such activities as charity care, health screening, community education about health risks, emergency room services, and basic research.[20] A hospital could satisfy the 1969 community-benefit requirement by offering emergency room services to all people regardless of their ability to pay, even if the hospital did not otherwise admit individuals who were unable to pay. In 1983, the IRS loosened the guidelines further when it specified that a nonprofit hospital could receive the federal income tax exemption even if it did not operate an emergency room.[21]

As a basis for comparison, the Catholic Health Association (CHA) recently released a set of guidelines for hospitals to use in identifying community benefits. CHA's guidelines, which are in some ways stricter than the IRS's standards, specify that community benefits should include services that are "offered to the broad community [and] designed to improve community health," and for which the hospital either is not compensated at all or is undercompensated relative to the costs of providing the service.[22] The CHA guidelines include charity care as a community benefit but specifically exclude bad debt.

PREVIOUS RESEARCH ON DIFFERENCES BETWEEN FOR-PROFIT AND NONPROFIT HOSPITALS

The Government Accountability Office recently released a report based on an analysis of hospitals in five selected states that compares the levels of uncompensated care provided by hospitals of different ownership types.[23] (The data on uncompensated care used for GAO's study are also used in this analysis.) GAO found that, in four of the five states analyzed, uncompensated care as a share of operating expenses was higher at nonprofit hospitals than at for-profit hospitals, although the differences were relatively small. A striking finding from that study was that (nonfederal) government hospitals devote a substantially greater share of their activities to uncompensated care than do either nonprofit or for-profit hospitals.[24]

Although other research findings besides the GAO report suggest that nonprofit hospitals provide higher levels of uncompensated care than do for-profits,[25] some researchers have concluded that the differences in the level of uncompensated care provided by nonprofit and for-profit hospitals are small.[26] Two studies have also reported that when nonprofit hospitals were acquired by for-profit corporations, they did not reduce their provision of uncompensated care or other community benefits.[27]

Although studies on uncompensated care often focus on the contrasts between for-profit and nonprofit hospitals, several factors may lead those different types of hospitals to provide similar levels of uncompensated care. First, both types of hospitals may choose to provide uncompensated care to maintain a good relationship with the local community. Second, some states, such as New Jersey, distribute funds to hospitals on the basis of the level of uncompensated care they provide, which can substantially reduce the financial disincentives to provide uncompensated care. And, third, regardless of nonprofit and for- profit hospitals' willingness to provide charity care, both types of hospitals may incur bad debt in the normal course of operations.

The difference in the level of uncompensated care provided by nonprofit and for-profit hospitals has generally been found to be small, but other disparities in hospitals' behavior have been documented. Nonprofit hospitals have been found by some researchers to be less efficient than for-profit hospitals, meaning that costs per unit of output are higher.[28] Many other studies report that nonprofits charge lower prices or markups than do for-profits.[29] Several studies have also concluded that for- profit hospitals appear to react more strongly than nonprofits do to the reimbursement environment by altering the mix of services they provide,[30] by limiting increases in the wages of hospital employees,[31] and by more aggressively coding services provided so as to increase reimbursement rates.[32] A large number of studies have examined differences in the quality of care and health outcomes between for-profit and nonprofit hospitals but have not generally identified any consistent patterns.[33]

STUDY DATA AND METHODS

The remainder of this paper assesses whether the three types of hospitals—nonprofit, for-profit, and government—provide different levels of community benefits. First, the types of services used in the analysis as measures of community benefits are explained. Next, the paper describes the data used to measure hospital characteristics and the provision of community benefits, and the analytical strategy used to compare hospitals of different ownership types. Then the results of the analysis are presented, which examine the differences between hospitals of different ownership types, both in their basic characteristics (size, location, and so on), and in their provision of community benefits.

Measures of Community Benefits

Because of the lack of general consensus on the definition of community benefits, many different types of services and activities could be regarded as community benefits. This analysis focuses on the provision of uncompensated care, the provision of Medicaid-covered services, and the provision of certain specialized facilities or services (burn intensive care, emergency room care, high-level trauma care, and labor and delivery services).

Although uncompensated care is the focus of this CBO paper and has frequently been analyzed by other researchers, it has substantial limitations as a measure of community benefits. The most significant limitation is that it does not distinguish between the provision of charity care for the indigent, which is more clearly a type of community benefit, and bad debt, which is not necessarily a community benefit. A hospital may incur bad debt when providing services to a high-income individual with insurance, for example, if the individual fails to pay the deductible for a hospital stay.[34]

Medicaid's payment rates have, in general, been found to be lower than the costs that hospitals incur for providing Medicaid-covered services. Providing hospital services to Medicaid patients is generally unprofitable and serves a needy population and can, therefore, be thought of as a type of community benefit. Like uncompensated care, however, the provision of Medicaid-covered services has significant limitations as a measure of community benefits. The profitability of providing care to Medicaid patients appears to vary widely from state to state and also probably varies from hospital to hospital, and from case to case. Because providing Medicaid-covered services is not always unprofitable, it is not always appropriate to treat it as a community benefit.

The four specialized services analyzed by CBO (burn intensive care, emergency room care, high-level trauma care, and labor and delivery services) were selected because they serve community needs and have been identified by other researchers as being generally unprofitable, and because data are readily available on which hospitals provide them.[35] CBO did not attempt directly to measure the profitability of each of the four specialized services.

Data Sources

Two data sets were constructed, the first including all Medicare-certified community hospitals in the United States and the second including only the subset of community hospitals for which data on uncompensated care were available. Both data sets include the following hospital characteristics: ownership status, specialized services provided, community characteristics, and financial characteristics. Sufficiently reliable data on uncompensated care were available only for hospitals in five states: California, Florida, Georgia, Indiana, and Texas. GAO, which gathered the data on uncompensated care, selected those states because they are geographically diverse, they have a large number of hospitals in each ownership group, and authorities in those states collected hospital- specific information on uncompensated care.[36]

GAO's measure of uncompensated-care costs is based on charges (or "list prices") deflated by a hospital-specific cost-to-charge ratio. The cost-to-charge ratio equals the total costs of providing care to all patients in a given hospital divided by the total charges for all patients in that hospital.[37]

The main source of data on hospital characteristics is the Medicare Hospital Cost Report database. All Medicare- certified hospitals in the United States must file an annual cost report with the Centers for Medicare & Medicaid Services (CMS). Medicare Hospital Cost Reports contain a wealth of information on providers, such as ownership type and facility characteristics, utilization data (discharges and days of patient care), costs and charges by cost center (in total, and for Medicare), and financial- statement data (including assets, revenues, and expenses).[38] The cost reports also provide information on the location of the hospitals, the number of beds in each facility, and the availability of three types of specialized patient services: emergency room care, burn intensive care, and labor and delivery services. To identify hospitals that provide high-level trauma care, CBO used an inventory of trauma centers provided by the Trauma Information Exchange Program (TIEP).[39]

The Medicare Hospital Cost Report data used in this analysis are from the March 2005 update, which includes all Medicare Hospital Cost Reports submitted up to that point. The analysis focuses on services provided in 2003, however, because the uncompensated-care data cover that period and because cost-report data are available for 2003 for over 4,500 community hospitals, representing nearly all such hospitals. Other hospital data are obtained from the "Provider Specific" file and the "Provider of Services" file, both maintained by CMS.

The characteristics of the county in which each hospital is located are taken from the 2004 Area Resource File, which is maintained by the Bureau of Health Professions of the Department of Health and Human Services. Those data include average per capita income in the county, the percentage of the population in poverty, the unemployment rate, and other population characteristics. Each hospital is associated with a set of population characteristics (income, and so on) based on the county in which that hospital is located. For each population characteristic, the most recent data available were used.

The level of uncompensated care provided by a hospital will depend, in part, on the size of the hospital, the characteristics of the community in which it is located, as well as the hospital's mission and form of organization. One of the reasons that nonprofit hospitals may provide a higher level of uncompensated care than for-profit hospitals do is simply that nonprofits tend to be larger than for-profits. To account for differences in hospitals' size in the comparison of levels of uncompensated care, CBO used uncompensated care as a share of operating expenses (the uncompensated-care share) as the main measure of uncompensated care.

Methods of Analysis

CBO used two approaches to compare the level of community benefits provided by the three different types of hospitals. The first approach is an "unadjusted" analysis that compares simple weighted averages among hospitals of different ownership types. The second approach is an "adjusted" analysis that measures the differences between hospitals of different ownership types, holding constant certain hospital characteristics, such as the size of the facility, the state in which it is located, and the income level of the community in which it is located. Those unadjusted and adjusted analyses were first applied to uncompensated-care shares, and then the same approach is used to analyze the provision of Medicaid-covered services, and the provision of certain specialized services.

The use of both unadjusted and adjusted analyses can help determine whether any observed differences among hospitals of different ownership types are attributable to the hospitals' location and size or to some other factor correlated with ownership status. As other researchers have pointed out, hospitals of different ownership types tend to be located in disparate geographic areas with divergent patient populations. One can think of different geographic areas as having varying levels of demand for uncompensated care, with low-income areas and areas with high numbers of uninsured people having higher levels of demand. The unadjusted uncompensated-care shares reflect both hospitals' willingness and ability to provide such care and their decision to locate in areas with high or low levels of demand for uncompensated care. The differences in adjusted uncompensated-care shares, by contrast, reflect differences in hospitals' willingness and ability to supply uncompensated care, after controlling for differences in the communities in which the hospitals are located and other hospital characteristics. Conceptually, the adjusted differences represent the differences that would occur if hospitals of all ownership types were located in the same areas and were the same in all respects other than ownership status.[40]

To calculate the adjusted differences in uncompensated- care shares, CBO regressed uncompensated-care shares on state indicator variables, local population characteristics, a measure of hospital size, case mix (in other words, the average intensity of illness and resource needs among a hospital's patients), and indicator variables for nonprofit and government ownership status.[41] ("For-profit" ownership is the omitted reference group.)[42] That regression yields adjusted differences in uncompensated-care shares for each state and the average for the entire five-state sample. That technical adjustment has the effect of correcting for differences in hospital size and local community characteristics that may affect the uncompensated-care share of a hospital, leaving a clearer picture of the differences in community benefits that are attributable solely to differences in ownership type.

CHARACTERISTICS OF HOSPITALS

Of the 4,518 community hospitals included in the national analysis, 58 percent (2,641) are categorized as nonprofit, 18 percent (794) as for-profit, and the remaining 24 percent (1,083) as government hospitals. Those different types of hospitals vary in their location, size, and financial performance, and in their provision of community benefits.

The distribution of hospital ownership varies markedly by region (see Table 2). In the Northeast, 89 percent of the hospitals are nonprofits, whereas in the South only 43 percent of the hospitals are nonprofits. For-profit hospitals are common in the South and West, but not in the Northeast and Midwest.

Table 2. Hospital Ownership Types, by Region

	Share of Hospitals (Percent)			Number of Hospitals of All Types
	Nonprofit	For-Profit	Government	
Northeast	89	6	5	618
Midwest	69	6	25	1,339
South	43	29	28	1,728
West	52	21	27	833
All Regions	58	18	24	4,518

Source: Congressional Budget Office based on the Medicare Hospital Cost Report, 2003.

Nonprofit hospitals tend to be larger than for-profit hospitals and are more likely to be teaching hospitals (see Table 3). The mean number of beds at nonprofit hospitals (164) is 26 percent larger than the mean number of beds at for-profits (130), and 82 percent larger than at government hospitals (90). The number of patient discharges and the number of employees (measured by full-time equivalents) follow similar patterns.

Teaching hospitals account for 31 percent of nonprofits versus 18 percent of for-profits and 13 percent of government hospitals.[43] The ratio of interns and residents to beds, a measure of teaching intensity, shows that nonprofit hospitals are involved to a greater degree in graduate medical education than are for-profits.[44] Nonprofits also have higher mean total assets, fixed assets, net patient revenues, and operating expenses than both for-profit and government hospitals. Nonprofit hospitals have a total margin (3.9 percent) that is somewhat higher than government hospitals' (2.9 percent) but lower than for- profits' (9.1 percent).[45]

Compared with for-profit hospitals and government hospitals, nonprofit hospitals tend to be located in counties with higher average incomes and lower poverty rates. Nonprofit hospitals also tend to be located in areas with relatively low rates of uninsurance and higher levels of education. Both nonprofit hospitals and government hospitals are more likely than for-profit hospitals to be located in rural areas.

Table 3. Characteristics of Hospitals, by Ownership Type

Hospital Characteristics	Ownership Type		
	For-Profit	Nonprofit	Government
Number of Hospitals in Data Set	794	2,641	1,083
Facility Size and Patient Population			
Number of hospital beds	130	164 ***	90 ***
Total discharges	5,666	8,337 ***	4,018 ***
Medicare discharges (Percent)	37.5	37.4	32.9 ***
Medicaid discharges (Percent)	16.9	13.5 ***	23.0 ***
Number of staff (Full-time equivalents)	465	955 ***	551 **
Case-mix index (Transfer-adjusted)	1.4	1.5 ***	1.4
SSI days as a percentage of Medicare days	13.2	8.1 ***	12.0 **
Hospital Characteristics			
Teaching hospital (Percent)	18.1	30.8 ***	12.8 ***
Ratio of interns/residents to (100) beds	3.5	12.2 ***	19.0 ***
Referral center (Percent)	3.8	5.9 **	4.0
Transplant center (Percent)	2.4	5.6 ***	3.7 *
Financial Measures			
Total assets (Millions of dollars)	57.0	137.2 ***	70.0 **
Fixed assets (Millions of dollars)	30.4	56.5 ***	26.6 *
Net patient revenue (Millions of dollars)	68.9	119.0 ***	58.6 **
Operating expenses (Millions of dollars)	64.5	120.6 ***	64.4
Total margin (Percent)[a]	9.1	3.9 [b]	2.9 [b]
Local Population Characteristics[c]			
Average per capita income (Dollars)	29,126	32,423 ***	29,273
Population in poverty (Percent)	13.4	11.4 ***	13.2
Population uninsured among people under age 65 (Percent)	19.0	15.4 ***	17.7 ***
Population eligible for Medicare (Percent)	14.4	14.9 ***	14.4
Unemployment rate	6.1	5.8 ***	6.0
Population with fewer than nine years of schooling (Percent)	9.3	7.0 ***	8.4 ***
Location			
Large urban area (Percent)	59.8	51.4 ***	24.1 ***
Small urban or suburban area (Percent)	33.1	34.3	41.8 ***
Rural area (Percent)	7.1	14.3 ***	34.1 ***

Source: Congressional Budget Office based on the Medicare Hospital Cost Report, 2003.

Notes: SSI = Supplemental Security Income.

All statistics represent means, unless otherwise noted.

The statistical significance was calculated for the differences between for-profit and nonprofit hospitals and between for-profit and government hospitals, using two-tailed Student's t-tests. * = $p<0.10$; ** = $p<0.05$; *** = $p<0.01$.

Approximately 700 hospitals were missing data on SSI days as a share of Medicare days and case-mix index. A small number of hospitals were missing data for some items.

Weights were used to calculate the following statistics: percentage of discharges (weight = discharges); case-mix index (weight =inpatient days); SSI days as a percentage of Medicare days (weight = Medicare days); ratio of interns/residents to (100) beds (weight = beds); local population characteristics (weight = inpatient days).

a. The source for total margins is the Medicare Payment Advisory Commission (MedPAC). Total margins were calculated by MedPAC among community hospitals paid under Medicare's prospective payment system in 2003.

b. Statistical significance not calculated.

c. Each hospital is assigned local population characteristics on the basis of the population of the county in which it is located.

DIFFERENCES IN THE PROVISION OF UNCOMPENSATED CARE

CBO's analysis of uncompensated care as a share of operating expenses was conducted using 1,057 community hospitals in the five selected states—California, Florida, Georgia, Indiana, and Texas—for which data on uncompensated care were available. Of those 1,057 community hospitals, 462 (44 percent) were nonprofit, 308 (29 percent) were for-profit, and 287 (27 percent) were government-owned. In the five states analyzed, nonprofit hospitals provided a total of about $3 billion in uncompensated care, government hospitals provided more than $3 billion, and for-profit hospitals provided about $1 billion in uncompensated care.

Table 4 presents the unadjusted uncompensated-care shares for each ownership type, as well as unadjusted and adjusted differences between nonprofit and for-profit hospitals, and between government hospitals and for-profit hospitals.[46] In the unadjusted results, nonprofit hospitals were found to devote a slightly larger share of their operating expenses to uncompensated care than did for-profits (a statistically significant difference of 4.7 percent versus 4.2 percent).

The adjusted differences in Table 4 reflect the estimated differences in uncompensated-care shares after controlling for the following variables: the hospital's size; the state in which it is located; the degree of urbanization of the community in which it is located; its case mix; the percentage of the surrounding county's population that lives in poverty; the percentage of the county's population that is uninsured; and the percentage of the county's population that is eligible for Medicare. (The full regression results used to generate the adjusted results in Table 4 are included in Table A-1.) After adjustment, the difference between nonprofit and for-profit hospitals in their average uncompensated-care share was a statistically significant 0.6

percentage points. As in the unadjusted results, government hospitals were found in the adjusted results to have much higher uncompensated-care shares than either nonprofit or for-profit hospitals. If nonprofit hospitals in the five selected states had behaved like otherwise similar for-profit hospitals—in other words, if they had provided the level of uncompensated care that CBO predicts would have been provided by otherwise similar for- profit hospitals—there is a 90 percent chance that nonprofit hospitals would have provided between $100 million and $700 million less in uncompensated care than they actually did provide.[47]

Table 4. Uncompensated-Care Shares, by Hospital Ownership Type and State

	Number of Hospitals	Mean Uncompensated-Care Share (Percent)			Difference between Nonprofit and For-Profit Hospitals (Percentage points)		Difference between Government and For-Profit Hospitals (Percentage points)	
		For-Profit	Non profit	Government	Unadjusted	Adjusted	Unadjusted	Adjusted
California	328	3.4	3.2	12.8	-0.2	-0.4	9.4 ***	8.1 ***
Florida	168	4.3	5.5	12.8	1.2 ***	0.9 *	8.5 ***	8.1 ***
Georgia	132	5.2	6.0	10.3	0.8	-0.4	5.1 ***	2.3
Indiana	97	1.9	3.9	3.4	1.9 ***	1.8 ***	1.5 ***	0.7
Texas	332	4.6	6.4	19.7	1.8 ***	2.1 **	15.2 ***	15.3 ***
All Five States	1,057	4.2	4.7	13.0	0.5 ***	0.6 *	8.9 ***	8.6 ***

Source: Congressional Budget Office based on the Medicare Hospital Cost Report, 2003, and data from the Government Accountability Office on uncompensated care.

Notes: The uncompensated-care share equals uncompensated-care costs as a share of total hospital operating expenses, expressed as a percentage. The adjusted differences reflect the differences between for-profit, nonprofit, and government hospitals after controlling for the following factors: number of hospital beds, hospital case mix, and population characteristics of the county in which the hospital was located (including percentage in poverty, percentage without insurance, percentage eligible for Medicare, and the degree of urbanization—large urban, suburban/small urban, or rural—of the county). In the "All Five States" model, state indicator variables were included, and each control variable was interacted with an indicator for the state in which the hospital was located. All regression models were weighted by operating expenses. Appendix A presents the regression models used to calculate the adjusted differences.

In the unadjusted results, the statistical significance of the differences (between for-profit and nonprofit hospitals and between for- profit and government hospitals) was calculated using two-tailed Student's t-tests. In the adjusted results, the statistical significance of the differences was calculated on the basis of the estimated regression coefficients and standard errors. * = $p<0.10$; ** = $p<0.05$; *** = $p<0.01$.

To check the sensitivity of the results to the particular empirical specification used, CBO analyzed a number of alternative specifications. Alternative models were considered that included only subsets of the control variables in the basic model (the results of two of those models are shown in the appendix); added a teaching-hospital control variable; used different functional forms for some of the variables; and used different geographic groupings (such as zip code) for defining certain variables (such as the poverty rate). In general, the key results on nonprofit ownership status were quite similar in those alternative analyses to the main results presented in Table 4. The finding that nonprofit hospitals in the five selected states have, on average, slightly higher uncompensated-care shares than for-profit hospitals appears, therefore, to be statistically robust, meaning that very similar key results occur when different analytical specifications are used.

Effect of Location on Adjusted Differences

The relatively small estimated differences that exist between nonprofit and for-profit hospitals in adjusted uncompensated-care shares could tend to mask larger differences in actual shares if nonprofits tended to be located in areas with high demand for uncompensated care. That is, the adjustment process controls for locational characteristics and would not, in a sense, give credit to nonprofit hospitals for their decision to operate in areas with a high demand for uncompensated care. On the basis of the national data presented in Table 3, however, it appears that nonprofit hospitals tend to be located in areas with relatively high income, low poverty rates, and low rates of uninsurance.[48]

To examine locational differences in more detail, CBO focused on the five states included in the uncompensated-care analysis and measured average per capita income, poverty rates, and rates of uninsurance in the counties where the hospitals were located (see Table 5). In each of the five states except for Indiana, nonprofit hospitals, compared with for-profit hospitals, were found to be located in counties with either lower poverty rates, lower rates of uninsurance, or both. (In Indiana, in comparison with for-profit hospitals, nonprofit hospitals were located in counties with higher rates of poverty and higher rates of uninsurance.) On the whole, nonprofit hospitals do not appear disproportionately to have characteristics, other than ownership type, that are associated with greater provision of uncompensated care. That fact results, in the analysis of uncompensated-care shares, in the unadjusted and adjusted differences between nonprofit and for-profit hospitals being quite similar.

Differences by State

States differ in whether they impose community-benefit requirements on nonprofit hospitals, in the strictness of those requirements, and in other factors that affect hospitals' provision of uncompensated care. The differences between nonprofit and for-profit hospitals in their uncompensated-care shares should not, therefore, be expected to be the same among different states.

In terms of community-benefit requirements, among the five states included in the uncompensated-care analysis, only California, Indiana and Texas require that nonprofit hospitals maintain and report community-benefit plans; only Texas and Indiana impose fines on nonprofit hospitals for not reporting community benefits; and only Texas requires that nonprofit hospitals demonstrate that they have met certain quantitative requirements in their provision of charity care and community benefits.

CBO's regression analysis of uncompensated-care shares allows for a separate comparison of nonprofit, for-profit, and government hospitals in each state. Those results, which appear in Table 4, show that in Florida nonprofit hospitals have somewhat higher uncompensated-care shares than otherwise similar for-profit hospitals (0.9 percentage points), while the differences between nonprofit and for-profit hospitals' uncompensated-care shares are larger in Indiana (1.8 percentage points) and Texas (2.1 percentage points).

Table 5. Economic Characteristics of Hospitals' Communities, by Hospital Ownership Type and State

	Number of Hospitals	Local Population Characteristics (Means)	Ownership Type		
			For-Profit	Nonprofit	Government
California	328	Average per capita income (Dollars)	32,221	32,673	31,264
		Population in poverty (Percent)	13.0	13.0	13.8
		Population uninsured among people under age 65 (Percent)	22.2	21.2 *	22.3
Florida	168	Average per capita income (Dollars)	29,491	28,731	29,036
		Population in poverty (Percent)	12.2	11.8	11.8
		Population uninsured among people under age 65 (Percent)	19.7	18.7 **	20.1
Georgia	132	Average per capita income (Dollars)	30,754	31,715	28,536
		Population in poverty (Percent)	14.8	13.1 **	15.0
		Population uninsured among people under age 65 (Percent)	17.8	17.6	17.9
Indiana	97	Average per capita income (Dollars)	27,571	28,356	27,788
		Population in poverty (Percent)	8.7	10.1 *	7.7
		Population uninsured among people under age 65 (Percent)	12.8	14.3 **	11.7 *
Texas	332	Average per capita income (Dollars)	28,347	29,580	27,483
		Population in poverty (Percent)	16.3	14.5 **	15.2
		Population uninsured among people under age 65 (Percent)	22.7	20.4 ***	21.3 *

Source: Congressional Budget Office.

Note: Each hospital was assigned local population characteristics on the basis of the population of the county in which it is located. The statistical significance was calculated for the differences between for-profit and nonprofit hospitals and between for-profit and government hospitals, using two-tailed Student's t-tests. * = $p<0.10$; ** = $p<0.05$; *** = $p<0.01$.

In California and Georgia, the differences in uncompensated-care shares between nonprofit and otherwise similar for-profit hospitals are not significantly different from zero. Given that the analysis of uncompensated-care shares includes only five states, it is not possible to draw any firm conclusions regarding possible links between state community-benefit requirements for nonprofit hospitals and the differences between nonprofit and for-profit hospitals in their uncompensated-care shares. It is worth noting, however, that among the five states examined, Texas and Indiana impose the strictest requirements on nonprofit hospitals, and the differences in uncompensated-care shares between nonprofit and for- profit hospitals appear to be largest in those two states.

Distribution of Hospitals' Uncompensated-Care Shares

The comparison of the mean uncompensated-care shares among hospitals of different ownership types masks substantial variation among individual hospitals. To illustrate the high degree of variation in uncompensated-care shares, CBO generated the histograms in Figure 1, which show the fraction of hospitals with different uncompensated-care shares by ownership type.[49] There is substantial variation within each ownership type in hospitals' uncompensated-care shares. Although nonprofit hospitals, on average, have higher uncompensated-care shares than do for-profits, the distributions of hospital-level uncompensated-care shares among those two types of hospitals overlap to a large extent. Among both nonprofit and for- profit hospitals, a large majority have either low uncompensated-care shares (below 5 percent) or moderate uncompensated-care shares (5 to 10 percent). Government hospitals on average provide much more uncompensated care than either nonprofit or for-profit hospitals, but a substantial share of government hospitals provides only modest levels of uncompensated care. The difference in the mean uncompensated-care shares between government hospitals and other types of hospitals is driven largely by the existence of a relatively small number of government hospitals—35 out of the 287 government hospitals in the five selected states—that had very high uncompensated-care shares (over 15 percent).

Differences in the Provision of Medicaid-Covered Services

Some industry experts and researchers include the so- called Medicaid shortfall as an additional type of community benefit. The Medicaid shortfall is the difference between the costs that hospitals incur as a result of providing services to Medicaid enrollees and Medicaid's payments to hospitals for those services. On the basis of data from the American Hospital Association, the

Lewin Group estimates that Medicaid's payments over the past several years have covered about 95 percent of the Medic-aid-related costs that hospitals incur.[50] Hospitals that treat a large number of Medicaid patients, therefore, are likely to face a larger Medicaid shortfall than hospitals that treat fewer Medicaid patients.

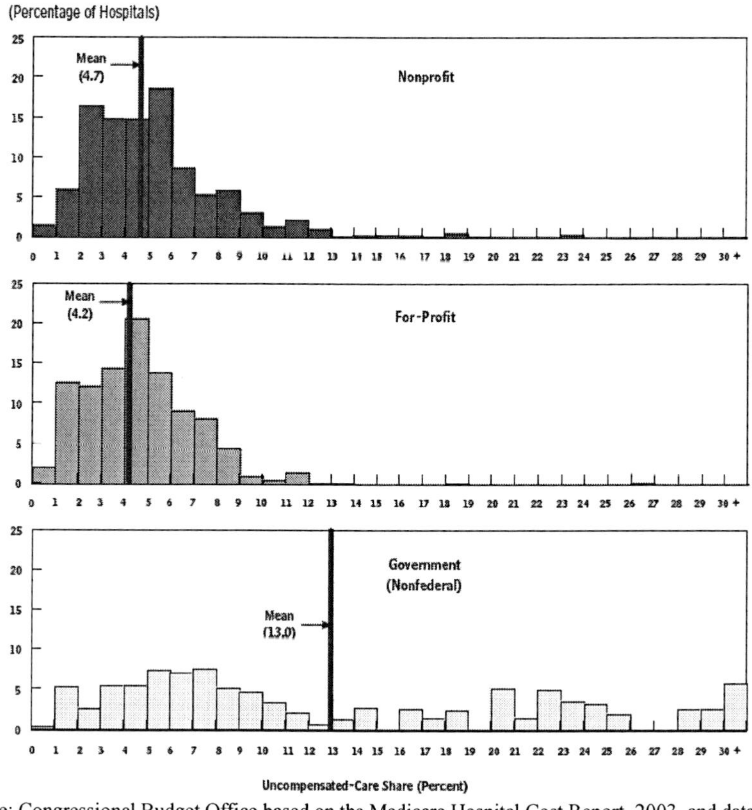

Source: Congressional Budget Office based on the Medicare Hospital Cost Report, 2003, and data from the Government Accountability Office on uncompensated care.

Note: "Government" hospitals include only nonfederal government-owned community hospitals.

The uncompensated-care share equals uncompensated-care costs as a share of total hospital operating expenses. Uncompensated- care shares are unadjusted. The bar height indicates the share of hospitals, in percent. The distributions are weighted by operating expenses and truncated at 30 percent. The solid vertical lines represent the weighted average uncompensated-care share for each ownership type.

Figure 1. Distribution of Hospitals, by Uncompensated-Care Share and by Ownership Type

To examine differences among nonprofit, for-profit, and government hospitals in the provision of care to Medicaid patients, CBO analyzed the

"Medicaid share," which is calculated for each hospital and equals the percentage of inpatient days accounted for by Medicaid patients. The Medicaid analysis included all community hospitals nationwide for which data were available (*N* = 4,397).[51] In 2003, the average Medicaid share among for-profit hospitals was 17.2 percent, among nonprofit hospitals it was 15.6 percent, and among government hospitals it was 27.0 percent (see Table 6). CBO calculated adjusted differences in Medicaid shares using regression models similar to those used to analyze the uncompensated-care share. After accounting for hospitals' characteristics and local population characteristics, CBO estimated that nonprofit hospitals had a Medicaid share that was 1.3 percentage points lower than for-profit hospitals, a difference that was statistically significant.

Table 6. Medicaid Shares, by Hospital Ownership Type

Mean Medicaid Share (Percent)			Difference between Nonprofit and for-Profit Hospitals (Percentage points)		Difference between Government and for-Profit Hospitals (Percentage points)	
For-Profit	Nonprofit	Government	Unadjusted	Adjusted	Unadjusted	Adjusted
17.2	15.6	27.0	-1.5 ***	-1.3 **	9.8 ***	8.8 ***

Source: Congressional Budget Office based on the Medicare Hospital Cost Report, 2003.

Notes: The Medicaid share equals Medicaid-covered hospital inpatient days as a share of total hospital inpatient days, expressed as a percentage. The adjusted values reflect the differences between for-profit and nonprofit hospitals, and between for-profit and government hospitals, after controlling for the state in which the hospital was located and the following factors: number of hospital beds, hospital case mix, and population characteristics of the county in which the hospital was located (including percentage in poverty, percentage without insurance, percentage eligible for Medicare, and the degree of urbanization—large urban, suburban/small urban, or rural—of the county). Each control variable was interacted with an indicator for the state in which the hospital was located. The regression model was weighted by operating expenses. Hospitals were excluded from the calculation of the adjusted differences if they were located in a state that did not have at least one for-profit hospital.

In the unadjusted results, the statistical significance of the differences (between for-profit and nonprofit hospitals, and between for- profit and government hospitals) was calculated using two-tailed Student's t-tests. In the adjusted results, the statistical significance of the differences was calculated on the basis of the estimated regression coefficients and standard errors. * = p<0.10; ** = p<0.05; *** = p<0.01.

The difference in Medicaid shares can be used to estimate the differences in the Medicaid shortfall as a share of operating expenses among different types of hospitals. On the basis of Lewin's estimated national average, the shortfall from treating Medicaid patients would equal about 5 percent of a hospital's Medicaid-related operating expenses. As a share of operating expenses, the Medicaid shortfall is estimated to be less than one-tenth of one percentage point higher at for-profit hospitals than at nonprofit hospitals. The fact that nonprofit hospitals tend to treat fewer Medicaid patients than otherwise similar for-profit hospitals implies that they probably face less of a Medicaid shortfall; but, as a share of operating expenses, the difference appears to be quite small.

DIFFERENCES IN THE PROVISION OF SPECIALIZED SERVICES

CBO analyzed the fraction of hospitals of different ownership types that provided the following specialized patient services: burn intensive care, emergency room care, high-level trauma care, and labor and delivery services (see Table 7).[52] Those services were selected because they have been identified by other researchers as being generally unprofitable. Like the analysis of Medicaid-covered services, the analysis of specialized services includes all community hospitals nationwide for which data were available (*N* = 4,397).[53]

In general, the analysis found that burn intensive care and high-level trauma care are provided by only a minority of hospitals, whereas a large majority of hospitals provide labor and delivery services, and nearly all hospitals provide emergency room care. On the basis of an analysis of the unadjusted fraction of hospitals providing each service, nonprofit hospitals were found to be significantly more likely than for-profit hospitals to provide each of the specialized services examined.

Adjusted differences in the provision of specialized services were also calculated using linear probability models that included the same set of control variables used in the regressions of uncompensated-care shares. After controlling for hospital characteristics and the characteristics of the local population, CBO found statistically significant differences between nonprofit hospitals and for-profit hospitals in the provision of two of the specialized services examined: nonprofit hospitals were 3.8 percentage points more likely to provide emergency room care, and they were 10.5 percentage points more likely to provide labor and delivery services. For each of the four specialized services, government hospitals were found in the adjusted results to be significantly more likely than otherwise similar for-profit hospitals to provide such services.

Table 7. Share of Hospitals That Provide Specialized Patient Services, by Hospital Ownership Type

	Share of Hospitals That Provide a Specialized Service (Percent)			Difference Between Nonprofit and For-Profit Hospitals (Percentage points)		Difference Between Government and For-Profit Hospitals (Percentage points)	
Specialized Service	For-Profit	Nonprofit	Government	Unadjusted	Adjusted	Unadjusted	Adjusted
Burn Intensive Care	1.0	6.8	22.0	5.8 ***	0.0	21.0 ***	19.9 ***
Emergency Room Care	96.6	98.5	97.1	1.9 ***	3.8 ***	0.6	4.9 ***
High-Level Trauma Care	9.3	33.0	48.0	23.8 ***	1.7	38.7 ***	25.9 ***
Labor and Delivery Services	72.2	83.5	86.5	11.3 ***	10.5 ***	14.3 ***	14.0 ***

Source: Congressional Budget Office based on data from the Medicare Hospital Cost Report, 2003, and the Trauma Information Exchange Program.

Notes: Providing "high-level trauma care" indicates that the hospital is a level 1 or level 2 adult trauma center (stand-alone pediatric trauma centers are not included). The adjusted values reflect the differences between for-profit and nonprofit hospitals and between for-profit and government hospitals, after controlling for the state in which the hospital was located and the following factors: number of hospital beds, hospital case mix, and population characteristics of the county in which the hospital was located (including percentage in poverty, percentage without insurance, percentage eligible for Medicare, and the degree of urbanization—large urban, suburban/ small urban, or rural—of the county). Each control variable was interacted with an indicator for the state in which the hospital was located. All regression models were weighted by operating expenses. Hospitals were excluded from the calculation of the adjusted differences if they were located in a state that did not include at least one for-profit hospital.

In the unadjusted results, the statistical significance of the differences (between for-profit and nonprofit hospitals, and between for- profit and government hospitals) was calculated using two-tailed Student's t-tests. In the adjusted results, the statistical significance of the differences was calculated on the basis of the estimated regression coefficients and standard errors. * = $p<0.10$; ** = $p<0.05$; *** = $p<0.01$.

For two of the specialized services that CBO examined— burn intensive care and high-level trauma care—the unadjusted results show that nonprofit hospitals were significantly more likely to provide those services than for-profit hospitals, but no statistically significant difference was found in the adjusted results. That fact implies that, compared with for-profit hospitals, nonprofit hospitals tend disproportionately to have characteristics other than ownership type that are associated with the provision of burn intensive care and high-level trauma care. Nonprofit hospitals, for example, tend to be larger than for-profit hospitals, and larger hospitals are more likely to provide burn intensive care and high-level trauma care.

LIMITATIONS OF THE ANALYSIS

Several important limitations apply to this analysis. First, the data on uncompensated care do not distinguish between charity care and bad debt. Charity care for the indigent is more clearly a type of community benefit, whereas bad debt is not necessarily a community benefit. Second, data on the amount of uncompensated care provided are available only for hospitals in five selected states. That limitation is attributable to the lack of a valid nationwide source of data on uncompensated care provided by hospitals. Hospitals in the five selected states are not necessarily representative of all hospitals nationwide. Third, the analysis of the Medicaid shortfall uses a single national estimate of the ratio of Medicaid's payments to hospitals' costs; the Medicaid shortfall varies among states and years and may also vary among individual hospitals. Fourth, the identification of certain types of specialized services as community benefits is based on a review of the literature and on the services that other researchers have identified. The value to the community of those services was not quantified by CBO and neither was their profitability.

A final limitation of the analysis relates to the interpretation of the reported differences in the level of community benefits provided by nonprofit and for-profit hospitals. Although the observed differences reflect the current differences in tax treatment, they may also reflect variations along other dimensions as well, such as organizational objectives.

APPENDIX: DETAILED RESULTS FROM REGRESSION MODELS OF UNCOMPENSATED-CARE SHARES

This appendix presents the results from three ordinary least squares (OLS) regression models.[54] In each of the three OLS models, the "uncompensated-care share"—uncompensated-care costs as a share of operating expenses—is used as the dependent variable, and the coefficients of interest are the indicator variables for the hospital ownership types. One of the models (the "full model") was used to estimate the adjusted differences in uncompensated-care shares, which are used as the main results of the uncompensated-care analysis (see Table 4 on page 15).[55] The other two models presented in this appendix are used as alternative specifications to examine the robustness of the main results.

The coefficient estimates shown in Table A-1 may be interpreted as percentage-point effects. For example, a coefficient estimate of 1 implies a 1 percentage-point increase in the predicted uncompensated-care share. The models pool hospitals in the five states for which uncompensated-care cost data are available and include state indicator variables and interactions of state indicator variables with each of the control variables. The key coefficients are the interactions of the state indicator variables with the indicators for nonprofit ownership status and government ownership status. (For-profit hospitals are the omitted reference group, which means that the coefficients on nonprofit ownership status and government ownership reflect an implicit comparison between those ownership types and for-profit hospitals.) The other control variables are as follows: the natural logarithm of the number of hospital beds, a measure of the hospital's case-mix index (missing values in the original data were set to zero); a variable indicating whether the case-mix index was missing (the case-mix index is missing for critical-access hospitals because they are not paid by Medicare under the case-mix-adjusted prospective payment system); the percentage of a county's population living in poverty; the percentage of a county population's that is uninsured; the percentage of a county's population that is eligible for Medicare; a location indicator for small urban or suburban counties; a location indicator for rural counties (large urban counties are the omitted reference group); and an indicator for state. Each of the control variables (other than the state indicators) is interacted with each state indicator variable, which allows the estimated effect of each control variable to vary from state to state.

The overall estimated effect of nonprofit ownership status and government ownership status on the uncompensated-care share is calculated by taking a weighted average of the five state-specific coefficients on the nonprofit indicators, where the weight equals each state's share of total hospital operating expenses among the five states. Those weighted averages are shown near the bottom of Table A-1.

Table A-1. Uncompensated-Care Shares (Ordinary least squares regression models)

Control Variable	Regression Model		
	Ownership	Ownership and Hospital Characteristics	Full Model (Ownership, hospital characteristics, and county characteristics)
Nonprofit Hospital Indicator			
California	-0.953 ***	-0.034	-0.369
Florida	1.379 ***	0.803	0.922 *
Georgia	1.830 ***	-0.927	-0.424
Indiana	-0.282	1.924 ***	1.790 ***
Texas	2.227 ***	1.833 **	2.060 **
Government Hospital Indicator			
California	8.609 ***	8.376 ***	8.117 ***
Florida	8.685 ***	7.834 ***	8.106 ***
Georgia	6.145 *	2.192 *	2.335
Indiana	-0.741 *	1.124 **	0.736
Texas	15.571 ***	14.672 ***	15.313 ***
Natural Logarithm of Hospital Beds			
California	n.a.	2.537 ***	2.933 ***
Florida	n.a.	1.479	0.777
Georgia	n.a.	5.030 *	4.798 *
Indiana	n.a.	0.042	0.339
Texas	n.a.	2.133 ***	1.625 **
Hospital Case-Mix Index			
California	n.a.	-9.616 ***	-10.344 ***
Florida	n.a.	-3.296	-2.252
Georgia	n.a.	-13.168 **	-13.672 **
Indiana	n.a.	-1.032	-1.267
Texas	n.a.	-4.913 **	-4.245 **

Table A-1 (Continued)

Indicator for Missing Case-Mix Index			
California	n.a.	-3.606	-5.004
Florida	n.a.	0.909	-0.558
Georgia	n.a.	-5.881	-7.586
Indiana	n.a.	0.306	0.142
Texas	n.a.	-7.179 **	-5.531 *
County Population in Poverty (Percent)			
California	n.a.	n.a.	0.162
Florida	n.a.	n.a.	0.164
Georgia	n.a.	n.a.	0.362
Indiana	n.a.	n.a.	0.040
Texas	n.a.	n.a.	0.254
County Population Uninsured (Percent)			
California	n.a.	n.a.	-0.210
Florida	n.a.	n.a.	0.037
Georgia	n.a.	n.a.	-0.488
Indiana	n.a.	n.a.	-0.195 **
Texas	n.a.	n.a.	-0.298
County Population Eligible for Medicare (Percent)			
California	n.a.	n.a.	0.005
Florida	n.a.	n.a.	-0.114 *
Georgia	n.a.	n.a.	-0.078
Indiana	n.a.	n.a.	0.003
Texas	n.a.	n.a.	0.037
Suburban/Small Urban Location Indicator			
California	n.a.	n.a.	2.065
Florida	n.a.	n.a.	-0.400
Georgia	n.a.	n.a.	-0.460
Indiana	n.a.	n.a.	0.393
Texas	n.a.	n.a.	-2.509 *
Rural Location Indicator			
California	n.a.	n.a.	-0.709
Florida	n.a.	n.a.	4.486 ***
Georgia	n.a.	n.a.	0.705
Indiana	n.a.	n.a.	2.568 *
Texas	n.a.	n.a.	-6.494 ***
State Indicator			
Florida	n.a.	-3.222	-2.682
Georgia	n.a.	-5.074	0.054
Indiana	n.a.	-0.839	-1.183
Texas	n.a.	-3.914	-0.836

Constant	4.157 ***	4.137	5.452
Memorandum:			
Weighted Average of Nonprofit Hospital Coefficient	0.625 ***	0.651 **	0.646 *
Weighted Average of Government Hospital Coefficient	9.200 ***	8.178 ***	8.571 ***
Number of Observations	1,058	1,058	1,057
R-Squared	0.433	0.509	0.527

Source: Congressional Budget Office.

Notes: The dependent variable in each model is the uncompensated-care share, which equals uncompensated-care costs as a share of total hospital operating expenses expressed as a percentage. The omitted reference categories are as follows: for-profit ownership, California, and urban location. At hospitals with missing values for case-mix index, the case-mix index is set to zero.* = $p<0.10$; ** = $p<0.05$; *** = $p<0.01$; n.a. = not applicable.

End Notes

[1] Hospitals are identified as nonprofit, for-profit, or governmental on the basis of classifications reported by hospitals in the "control type" variable in the Medicare Hospital Cost Report. According to the control type variable, "nonprofit" refers to voluntary nonprofit (with or without church affiliation); "for-profit" refers to proprietary hospitals owned by individuals, corporations, partnerships, or other entities; and "government" refers to state, county, city-county, city, hospital-district, or other governmental entities (federal hospitals were excluded from the analysis).

[2] "Community hospitals" include nonfederal short-term general hospitals. This definition includes most hospital facilities but excludes, for example, federal hospitals run by the Veterans Administration, psychiatric hospitals, and long-term-care hospitals. Several of the key data sources used are Medicare administrative files. Therefore, only Medicare-certified community hospitals were included in the analyses in this paper. Throughout the text "all community hospitals" refers to all Medicare-certified community hospitals. The findings are referred to as representing the year 2003, but the data are actually taken from either 2003 or 2002. For the analysis of uncompensated care, which includes hospitals in only five states, the data for 57 percent of hospitals are from federal fiscal year (FFY) 2003, and those for 43 percent of hospitals are from FFY 2002. For convenience, 2003 is used to describe the findings because the majority of hospitals report data for FFY 2003. For consistency, the analysis for all community hospitals used the same data years that were used to analyze uncompensated care costs in the five states. The FFY 2003 data were used for all hospitals not in the five states. For the other analyses, which include hospitals in all of the states, 90 percent of hospitals had FFY 2003 data and 10 percent of hospitals had FFY 2002 data.

[3] See Statement of David M. Walker, Comptroller General of the United States, before the House Committee on Ways and Means, published as Government Accountability Office, *Nonprofit, For- Profit, and Government Hospitals: Uncompensated Care and Other Community Benefits*, GAO-05-743T (May 26, 2005), available at www.gao.gov/new.items/d05743t.pdf.

[4] The range of $100 million to $700 million represents the 90 percent confidence interval from the underlying statistical analysis.

[5] In CBO's analysis, a hospital provides "high-level trauma care" if it is a level 1 or level 2 adult trauma center (stand-alone pediatric trauma centers are not included). A hospital may be designated as a trauma center if it meets certain criteria developed by the American College of Surgeons. Trauma centers are assigned a level ranging from 1 through 5, with level 1 being the highest. To be designated a level 1 or level 2 trauma center, a hospital must "[provide] comprehensive trauma care" and must "have immediate availability of trauma surgeons, anesthesiologists, physician specialists, nurses, and resuscitation equipment." See Ellen J. MacKenzie and others, "National Inventory of Hospital Trauma Centers," *Journal of the American Medical Association*, vol. 289, no. 12 (March 26, 2003), pp. 1515-1522.

[6] The terms "nonprofit" and "tax-exempt" (or "untaxed") are sometimes used interchangeably, but they are technically distinct. For the purposes of federal taxation, an organization may be deemed tax-exempt by meeting the requirements of section 501 of the Internal Revenue Code. Nonprofit status, on the other hand, is granted by state governments on the basis of criteria that vary from state to state. In CBO's analysis, hospitals that identify themselves as nonprofit in Medicare Hospital Cost Reports are assumed to be exempt from federal, state, and local taxes.

[7] Burton A. Weisbrod, *The Nonprofit Economy* (Cambridge, Mass.: Harvard University Press, 1988).

[8] A concept in the discipline of economics that is similar to a collective good is that of a "public good." Public goods are defined as having two properties: (1) nonrivalry in consumption (meaning that one person's consumption does not diminish another person's ability to consume the same good) and (2) nonexcludability (meaning that, because of the nature of the good, it is not feasible, once the good has been produced, to stop someone from consuming it; therefore, it is not possible for a seller of the good to recoup adequate payment for it). If nonindigent members of the community are made better off when indigent individuals are given health care, and if it is not possible for the hospital that provides such care to prevent nonindigent community members who have not contributed to the hospital from being made better off, then the provision of uncompensated care to poor people fits the definition of a public good. Because people can benefit from a public good without paying anything toward its production, a private marketplace may not produce an appropriate amount of such goods. Governments may intervene to bring about adequate production of public goods by either having the government produce those goods or by providing subsidies to private producers of such goods. Prevention of the spread of communicable disease also fits the definition of a public good and provides an additional rationale for subsidization of certain hospital activities, including care for the indigent.

[9] For details on Texas's charity-care standards for the nonprofit hospital tax exemption, see Statement of David M. Walker, May 26, 2005; and Kathryn J. Jervis, "A Review of State Legislation and a State Legislator Survey Related to Not-for-Profit Hospital Tax Exemption and Health Care for the Indigent," *Journal of Health Care Finance*, vol. 32, no. 2 (Winter 2005), pp. 36-71.

[10] See Congressional Budget Office, *Nonprofit Hospitals and Tax Arbitrage* (December 2006).

[11] See Joint Committee on Taxation, *Estimates of Federal Tax Expenditures for Fiscal Years 2006-2010*, JCS-2-06 (2006).

[12] For-profit hospitals also face an incentive to minimize their tax burden, but they are constrained from doing so by their owners' interests in generating and distributing income.

[13] See Congressional Budget Office, *Taxing the Untaxed Business Sector* (July 2005).

[14] Medicare DSH payments are based on each hospital's share of low-income patients. For the purposes of determining Medicare DSH payments, each hospital's disproportionate patient percentage is calculated, which equals the share of Medicare patient days accounted for by Medicare beneficiaries who receive Supplemental Security Income plus Medicaid patient

days as a share of total patient days. The mechanism for allocating Medicaid DSH funds varies from state to state.

[15] If a Medicare beneficiary does not pay the required deductible or coinsurance for a hospital stay, the hospital may, under certain conditions, report the unpaid amounts as bad debt and receive reimbursement from Medicare for 70 percent of that bad debt. See Statement of Mark McClellan, Administrator of the Centers for Medicare & Medicaid Services, *Tax Exemption for Hospitals and Federal Payment for Uncompensated Care*, before the House Committee on Ways and Means (May 26, 2005), available at www.cms.hhs.gov/media

[16] Many states use Medicaid supplemental payment programs, including DSH and upper payment limit (UPL) arrangements, to "recycle" Medicaid funds in order to increase the federal matching contribution. Those recycling strategies result in much of Medicaid's DSH funding not being retained by hospitals and, instead, being returned to states through provider taxes or intergovernmental transfers. One recent study estimated that only roughly half of the total spending on Medicaid DSH was retained by hospitals, with the rest paid back to states or retained by states. See Teresa A. Coughlin, Brian K. Bruen, and Jennifer King, "States' Use of Medicaid UPL and DSH Financing Mechanisms," *Health Affairs*, vol. 23, no. 2 (March/April 2004), pp. 245-257. The effective subsidy to hospitals from Medicaid DSH spending, therefore, is substantially less than the $9 billion in total spending on Medicaid DSH. UPL arrangements result in payments that, on the basis of Coughlin's study, appear in large part to be returned to the states rather than retained by hospitals. UPL payments are, therefore, not listed in this section as a type of subsidy for hospitals.

[17] See Jack Hadley and John Holahan, "How Much Medical Care Do the Uninsured Use, and Who Pays for It?," *Health Affairs*, Web Exclusive (February 12, 2003), Exhibit 4, p. 76.

[18] Joel Weissman, "Uncompensated Hospital Care: Will It Be There if We Need It?," *Journal of the American Medical Association*, vol. 276, no. 10 (September 11, 1996), pp. 823-828.

[19] Internal Revenue Service, Revenue Ruling 56-185, 1956-1 C.B. 202, available at www.irs.gov/pub/irs-tege/rr56-185.pdf.

[20] Internal Revenue Service, Revenue Ruling 69-545, 1969-2 C.B. 117, available at www.irs.gov/pub/irs-tege/rr69-545.pdf.

[21] Internal Revenue Service, Revenue Ruling 83-157, 1983-2 C.B. 94, available at www.irs.gov/pub/irs-tege/rr83-157.pdf.

[22] Catholic Health Association, *A Guide for Planning and Reporting Community Benefit*, available at www.chausa.org/NR/rdonlyres/ 7E5CFBD9-F741-4BA6-A74C-E8F14EC9DF82/0/ReferenceI.pdf.

[23] Statement of David M. Walker, May 26, 2005.

[24] A 1990 GAO study also found that government hospitals devoted a larger share of their activities to uncompensated care than either nonprofit or for-profit hospitals. See General Accounting Office, *Nonprofit Hospitals: Better Standards Needed for Tax Exemption*, GAO/HRD-90-84 (May 30, 1990), available at http://archive. gao.gov/d24t8/141681.pdf. The difference in uncompensated- care shares between government hospitals and other hospitals appears to have grown substantially since the late 1980s.

[25] Mark Schlesinger and others, "Competition, Ownership and Access to Hospital Services," *Medical Care*, vol. 35, no. 9 (1997), pp. 974-992.

[26] Frank A. Sloan, "Not-for-Profit Ownership and Hospital Behavior," in A.J. Culyer and J.P. Newhouse, eds., *Handbook of Health Economics* (Amsterdam: Elsevier Science B.V., 2000); and Statement of Mark B. McClellan, May 26, 2005.

[27] Gary J. Young, Kamal R. Desai, and Carol Van Deusen Lukas, "Does the Sale of Nonprofit Hospitals Threaten Health Care for the Poor?," *Health Affairs*, vol. 16, no. 1 (January/February 1997), pp. 137-141; and Gary J. Young and Kamal R. Desai, "Nonprofit Hospital Conversions and Community Benefits: New Evidence from Three States," *Health Affairs*, vol. 18, no. 5 (September/ October 1999), pp. 146-155.

[28] George W. Wilson and Joseph M. Jadlow, "Competition, Profit Incentives, and Technical Efficiency in the Provision of Nuclear Medicine Services," *Bell Journal of Economics*, vol.

13, no. 2 (Autumn 1982), pp. 472-482; Regina E. Herzlinger and William S. Krasker, "Who Profits from Nonprofits?," *Harvard Business Review*, vol. 93 (1987), pp. 93-106; and David M. Cutler and Jill R. Horwitz, "Converting Hospitals from Not-for-Profit to For-Profit Status: Why and What Effects?," in D.M. Cutler, ed., *The Changing Hospital Industry: Comparing Not-for-Profit and For-Profit Institutions* (Chicago: University of Chicago Press, 2000). Note, however, that at least one study has found that nonprofit hospitals are more efficient than for-profit hospitals. See Stephen Zuckerman, Jack Hadley, and Lisa Iezzoni, "Measuring Hospital Efficiency with Frontier Cost Functions," *Journal of Health Economics*, vol. 13 (1994), pp. 255-280.

[29] Craig G. Coelen, "Hospital Ownership and Comparative Hospital Costs," in Bradford H. Gray, ed., *For-Profit Enterprise in Health Care* (Washington, D.C.: National Academy Press, 1986); Robert V. Pattison and Hallie M. Katz, "Investor-Owned and Not-for-Profit Hospitals: A Comparison Based on California Data," *New England Journal of Medicine*, vol. 309 (1983), pp. 347-353; Robert V. Pattison, "Response to Financial Incentives Among Investor-Owned and Not-for-Profit Hospitals: An Analysis Based on California Data 1978-82, in Gray, ed., *For-Profit Enterprise in Health Care*; and Richard G. Frank and David S. Salkever, "Nonprofit Organization in the Health Sector," *Journal of Economic Perspectives*, vol. 8, no. 4 (Autumn 1994), pp. 129- 144.

[30] Jill R. Horwitz, "Making Profits and Providing Care: Comparing Nonprofit, For-Profit, and Government Hospitals," *Health Affairs*, vol. 24, no. 3 (May/June 2005), pp. 790-801.

[31] Daniel P. Kessler and Mark B. McClellan, "The Effects of Hospital Ownership on Medical Productivity," *Rand Journal of Economics*, vol. 33, no. 3 (Autumn 2002), pp. 488-506.

[32] Elaine Silverman and Jonathan Skinner, "Medicare Upcoding and Hospital Ownership," *Journal of Health Economics*, vol. 23, no. 2 (March 2004), pp. 369-389; and Leemore S. Dafny, "How Do Hospitals Respond to Price Changes?," *American Economic Review*, vol. 95, no. 5 (December 2005), pp. 1525-1547.

[33] Frank A. Sloan and others, "Hospital Ownership and Cost and Quality of Care: Is There a Dime's Worth of Difference?," *Journal of Health Economics*, vol. 21, no. 1 (January 2001), pp. 1-21; Edmund R. Becker and Frank A. Sloan, "Hospital Ownership and Performance," *Economic Inquiry*, vol. 23, no. 1 (January 1985), pp. 21-36; Gary Gaumer, "Medicare Patient Outcomes and Hospital Organizational Mission," in Gray, ed., *For-Profit Enterprise in Health Care*; Stephen M. Shortell and Edward F. X. Hughes, "The Effects of Regulation, Competition, and Ownership on Mortality Rates Among Hospital Inpatients," *New England Journal of Medicine*, vol. 318, no. 17 (1988), pp. 1100-1107; Emmett B. Keeler and others, "Hospital Characteristics and Quality of Care," *Journal of the American Medical Association*, vol. 268, no. 13 (1992), pp. 1709-1714; Sloan, "Not-for-Profit Ownership and Hospital Behavior"; and Kessler and McClellan, "The Effects of Hospital Ownership on Medical Productivity."

[34] There is very little direct evidence on the income and insurance status of the patients who account for hospitals' uncompensated care. Two surveys of uncompensated-care patients, both limited to hospitals in Massachusetts, showed that most uncompensated care was attributable to uninsured patients (see Joel S. Weissman, Carol Van Deusen Lukas, and Arnold M. Epstein, "Bad Debt and Free Care in Massachusetts Hospitals," *Health Affairs*, vol. 11, no. 2, Summer 1992, pp. 148-161), and that the great majority of bad debt was attributable to patients with incomes below 200% of the federal poverty line (see Joel S. Weissman, Paul Dryfoos, and Katharine London, "Income Levels of Bad-Debt and Free-Care Patients in Massachusetts Hospitals," *Health Affairs*, vol. 18, no. 4, July/August 1999, pp. 156-166). Those findings support the validity of the use of uncompensated care as a measure of community benefits, but they are not necessarily generalizable nationwide.

[35] William M. Gentry, and John R. Penrod, "The Tax Benefits of Not-for-Profit Hospitals," in D.M. Cutler, ed., *The Changing Hospital Industry: Comparing Not-for-Profit and For-Profit Institutions* (Chicago: University of Chicago Press, 2000); and Horwitz, "Making Profits and Providing Care: Comparing Nonprofit, For-Profit, and Government Hospitals."

Gentry and Penrod point out that emergency room care and labor and delivery services are financially unrewarding to hospitals because they are provided to disproportionately large numbers of Medicaid enrollees and the uninsured. Also, the Emergency Medical Treatment & Active Labor Act (EMTALA) makes the provision of emergency room care less financially attractive to hospitals. Complying with EMTALA, which is a precondition for participation in the Medicare program, requires that hospitals if they choose to offer emergency room care—provide screening and stabilization services to all patients entering the emergency room regardless of their ability to pay. Some specialized services, besides the four CBO examined, have also been identified as generally unprofitable, but data on which hospitals provided those other services were not readily available.

[36] For-profits hospitals had a larger market share in the five GAO states than in states not included in the GAO data. Among the hospitals included in the GAO data, 29 percent were for-profit, while among the hospitals that were included in the national analysis but not in the five GAO states only 14 percent were for-profit. That difference in for-profit market share implies that it may be difficult to generalize findings from the five GAO states to the national level.

[37] Cost-to-charge ratios vary widely across hospitals, with ratios ranging from 0.17 (the 5th percentile) to 0.70 (the 95th percentile).

[38] Although the Medicare Hospital Cost Report includes some information on uncompensated care, CBO did not analyze those Cost Report-based data because of concerns over the quality and consistency of the data. Nancy M. Kane and Stephen A. Magnus present a detailed description of the limitations of the Medicare Cost Report, especially financial measures contained in the cost report's worksheet G and uncompensated care in worksheet S-10. See Nancy M. Kane and Stephen A. Magnus, "The Medicare Cost Report and the Limits of Hospital Accountability: Improving Financial Accounting Data," *Journal of Health Politics, Policy and Law*, vol. 26, no. 1 (February 2001), pp. 81-105.

[39] National Inventory of Trauma Centers Database (Upper Marlboro, Md.: American Trauma Society-Trauma Information Exchange Program, 2006), accessed October 4, 2006. The analysis and interpretation of the data on high-level trauma care presented in this paper are solely the responsibility of CBO and do not represent the views or conclusions of TIEP, its funders, or those who carried out the original collection of the data.

[40] Nonprofit hospitals operating in the same market as for-profits appear to imitate their behavior to some extent. See Cutler and Horwitz, "Converting Hospitals from Not-for-Profit to For-Profit Status: Why and What Effects?"; Silverman and Skinner, "Medicare Upcoding and Hospital Ownership"; and Jonathan Gruber, "The Effects of Competitive Pressure on Charity-Hospital Response to Price Shopping in California," *Journal of Health Economics*, vol. 13, no. 2 (1994), pp. 183-212. That phenomenon has led some researchers to focus not on the effect of the ownership status of individual hospitals, but, instead, on the effect of the share of hospitals that are for-profit in defined geographic areas. See, for example, Mark Duggan, "Hospital Market Structure and the Behavior of Not-for-Profit Hospitals," *Rand Journal of Economics*, vol. 33, no. 3 (Autumn 2002), pp. 433-446. CBO did not analyze any market-level ownership effects or interaction effects among hospitals. Possible interaction effects might include crowding out (the existence of governmental hospitals could reduce the uncompensated care provided by nongovernmental hospitals in the same market) and imitation effects.

[41] An indicator variable is one that only takes on values of either zero or one. For example, the state indicator variable for Alaska equals one for all hospitals located in Alaska and zero for all other hospitals.

[42] In the uncompensated-care-share regressions, each independent variable is interacted with—in other words, multiplied by—a set of indicator variables representing the state in which the hospital is located. That allows the estimated effect of each independent variable to vary from state to state. The uncompensated-care-share regressions are weighted by operating expenses.

[43] In this analysis, a teaching hospital is defined as a hospital that reports being a teaching hospital in the Medicare Hospital Cost Report.

[44] Some researchers treat the costs that hospitals incur in providing graduate medical education as a type of community benefit, similar to the provision of uncompensated care. Others have argued that medical residents bear the costs of their own training by earning salaries less than the revenue generated for the hospital by the services they provide, and that medical residents ultimately benefit from their training when they receive the higher salaries they can command because of that training. Teaching hospitals also receive payments from Medicare on the basis of the number of residents in training. Those facts imply that providing graduate medical education is not necessarily unprofitable for the teaching hospital and does not necessarily meet the criteria CBO used to identify services as community benefits.

[45] The total margin is defined as the excess of total payments from all sources over all costs as a share of payments.

[46] The unadjusted uncompensated-care shares reported by CBO inTable 4 differ slightly from the uncompensated-care shares reported by GAO (see Statement of David M. Walker, May 26, 2005, "Highlights" and p. 11). The discrepancy is attributable to the use of different data sources for hospital operating expenses (hospital operating expenses are used as the denominator in the calculation of uncompensated-care shares). The differences in total operating expenses between the two data sources are relatively small and are not large enough to substantially affect the key results.

[47] The range of $100 million to $700 million represents the 90 percent confidence interval from the underlying statistical analysis.

[48] At the national level, nonprofit hospitals, compared with for- profit hospitals, tend to be located in higher-income counties (see Table 3). That fact is partly attributable to regional differences and the uneven distribution of hospitals across regions (see Table 2). In the Northeast, a region with relatively high incomes, nonprofits account for 89 percent of all hospitals and for-profits account for only 6 percent. In the South, a region with relatively low incomes, nonprofits account for 43 percent of all hospitals, and for-profits account for 29 percent. Those regional differences in income can account for much of the observed differences between nonprofit and for-profit hospitals in the average income and poverty rates of the communities they serve.

[49] To generate the histograms in Figure 1, unadjusted uncompensated-care shares are used and each hospital is weighted by its operating expenses.

[50] Al Dobson and others, *Executive Summary: Evaluation of the Adequacy of Medicaid Payments to Hospitals in Pennsylvania* (prepared by the Lewin Group for the Hospital and Healthsystem Association of Pennsylvania, June 2005), available at www.haponline.org/downloads/Evaluation_of_the_Adequacy_of_Medicaid_Payments_to_Hospitals_in_Pennsylvania_LEWIN_Exec_Summ. pdf.

[51] Hospitals were excluded from the calculation of the adjusted differences in Medicaid shares if they were located in a state that did not have at least one for-profit hospital. The four states that did not meet this criterion lacked adequate comparison groups and could not, therefore, be used to estimate differences between for- profit hospitals and other ownership types.

[52] Data on burn intensive care, emergency room care, and labor and delivery services were taken from the Medicare Hospital Cost Report and are from 2003. Data on high-level trauma care are from 2006.

[53] Hospitals were excluded from the calculation of the adjusted differences in the provision of specialized services if they were located in a state that did not have at least one for-profit hospital. The four states that did not meet this criterion lacked adequate comparison groups and could not, therefore, be used to estimate differences between for-profit hospitals and other ownership types. As a specification check, CBO also estimated adjusted differences in the provision of specialized services excluding any state in which there was no variation among hospitals in the provision of the specialized service (in some states, for example, all

hospitals provide emergency room care). The key results from that alternative analysis were very similar to the results presented in Table 7.

[54] OLS models provide estimates of the relationship between an outcome of interest, referred to generically as the "dependent" variable, and a set of variables—referred to as "control" (or, "independent") variables—thought to influence the outcome of interest.

[55] The adjusted differences reflect the association between uncompensated-care shares and nonprofit ownership status and between uncompensated-care shares and government ownership status, after controlling for characteristics of hospitals other than ownership status.

In: Nonprofit Hospitals and the Community… ISBN: 978-1-61761-999-1
Editor: Maria G. Reyes

Chapter 4

NONPROFIT HOSPITALS AND TAX ARBITRAGE

Congressional Budget Office

SUMMARY

The federal government exempts nonprofit hospitals from federal income taxation and allows them to issue tax-exempt debt. To qualify for those tax advantages, the hospitals must provide community benefits, which the Internal Revenue Service (IRS) defines as promoting the health of any broad class of people, perhaps including such activities as charity care, health screening, community education about health risks, emergency room services, and basic research. In effect, nonprofit hospitals are thus required to provide services that may differ somewhat from those provided by for- profit hospitals. Analysts and policymakers have questioned, however, the degree to which the activities of nonprofit and for-profit hospitals actually differ and whether any resulting community benefits are sufficient to justify the tax benefits that non-profits receive.

This analysis by the Congressional Budget Office (CBO) documents the magnitude of the tax advantages provided to nonprofit hospitals as a result of their exemption from corporate income taxes and their ability to issue tax-exempt debt.[1] According to the Joint Committee on Taxation (JCT), the exemption from income taxes provided nonprofit hospitals with about $2.5

billion in tax savings in 2002 (the most recent year for which such a calculation can be made), and the use of tax-exempt bonds provided them $1.8 billion—$4.3 billion that substantially reduced their cost of capital. Those advantages represented a transfer of resources from federal taxpayers to non-profit hospitals.[2] Nonprofit hospitals may use such resources in several ways. Some of those resources, as intended, may finance community benefits, such as reducing the prices of hospital services, providing charity care, or educating the community about health risks. Some may turn out to be transfers to providers, perhaps allowing higher compensation for employees, for instance. Finally, some of the resources may be wasted by inducing nonprofit hospitals to make less productive use of capital. For example, their lower cost of capital may induce investment in projects with relatively low pretax returns, thereby reallocating resources from more productive private-sector investments.

The analysis then examines one way to reduce the tax advantages: broaden the definition of tax arbitrage and thereby reduce the amount of tax-exempt debt that nonprofit hospitals would issue. Many nonprofit institutions, including hospitals, use tax- exempt debt to finance buildings and equipment that they could have financed by selling their own investment assets. Their decisions to finance operating assets with tax-exempt debt are influenced by their ability to earn an untaxed return on their investment assets that is higher than the interest cost they must pay on the tax-exempt debt.

That earnings differential could be characterized as a type of tax arbitrage. As administered, the existing rules in the tax code and the Department of the Treasury's regulations limit tax arbitrage by restricting the yield on a bond issuer's investments. Specifically, the yield can be no higher than the interest cost on the tax-exempt bonds if the bond proceeds are used to finance investment assets or if other assets are used to replace the bond proceeds (replacement proceeds), such as assets that are pledged as security for the bond issue.[3] The analysis examines the implications of broadening the definition of tax arbitrage to include earnings from assets not currently considered to be replacement proceeds but that nonetheless contribute indirectly to securing the bonds.

Of the 348 hospitals that borrowed in 2002 using tax-exempt debt, CBO estimated the amount of arbitrage bonds based on that broader definition for 310, the ones for which complete data were available. At the time they borrowed, about 80 percent of those hospitals were earning returns from that broader form of tax arbitrage on 60 percent of their outstanding stock of tax-exempt bonds. (See Appendix A for arbitrage estimates for all 1,276 hospitals that had tax-exempt debt on their balance sheets in 2002.) The estimates of tax arbitrage decline if the definition is narrowed to allow hospitals to set aside some investment assets as precautionary savings, which are not subject to yield restriction. If such savings amount to 100 days of operating expenses, for example (the median was 117 days in 2002), 35 percent of those 310 hospitals that borrowed in 2002 were earning returns from arbitrage on 33 percent of their outstanding stock of tax-exempt bonds.

If a broader definition of arbitrage was implemented and nonprofit hospitals continued accumulating assets and borrowing as they had in the past, their new bond issues would tend to exhaust the assets subject to yield restriction. Eventually, the hospitals would reach a steady state between accumulating assets and tax-exempt borrowing, and the prevalence of tax arbitrage for new issues of tax-exempt bonds would be lower than when the broader definition was first adopted. For example, without an allowance for precautionary savings, 37 percent of the 310 hospitals that borrowed using tax-exempt debt in 2002 would have the yield restricted on 28 percent of the dollar value of those new bond issues. If regulations allowed precautionary savings for 100 days of operating expenses, 15 percent of hospitals would have the yield restricted on 9 percent of their new bond issues. If the behavior of the 310 hospitals that borrowed in 2002 was typical, the estimates for hospitals that borrow in the future would probably be similar.

Over time, a broadened definition of tax arbitrage would improve the federal government's net fiscal condition. Hospitals would have to reduce their new issues of tax- exempt bonds (either reducing investment in operating assets or switching to taxable debt) by 28 percent (or by 9 percent if the policy accommodated precautionary savings). For example, if tax-exempt bonds provide $1.8 billion in annual tax benefits to nonprofit hospitals, as estimated for 2002, over time the broadened definition of tax arbitrage would save $504 million per year (or $162 million if allowance was made for precautionary savings). If hospitals chose instead to subject their investment assets to yield restriction, the federal government's forgone tax revenues would not change but the government would realize an equivalent amount in reduced borrowing costs or rebates of excess yields.

THE COSTS AND BENEFITS OF NONPROFIT HOSPITALS' TAX PREFERENCES

Nonprofit hospitals are more common than for-profit hospitals. In 2003, for example, 59 percent of community hospitals providing short-term care were nonprofit, and 18 percent were for-profit (the other 23 percent were government-owned). Nonprofits thus accounted for about 77 percent of private community hospitals. Nonprofits accounted for an even larger share of the fixed assets owned by private hospitals—86 percent—indicating that nonprofit hospitals are, on average, somewhat larger than for-profits.

The federal tax system treats nonprofit hospitals favorably in several ways. For-profit hospitals pay corporate income taxes on their net income, but nonprofit hospitals pay no taxes on their net income. In addition, the interest income earned by businesses and individuals that purchase the debt issued by for-profit hospitals is subject to federal corporate and individual income taxation, whereas the interest income earned on debt issued by state and local governments on behalf of nonprofit hospitals is generally exempt from those taxes. Nonprofit hospitals also benefit from the deductibility of charitable contributions and from their exemption from state and local corporate income taxes, local property taxes, and sales tax on their purchases.

The Internal Revenue Service's regulations require that, in exchange for such favorable tax treatment, nonprofit hospitals must promote the health of any broad class of people.[4] Those services can take a variety of forms: conducting basic research, health screening, and educational outreach (which are not commonly provided in private markets) and providing hospital services comparable to those at for-profits but at below-market prices or for free, such as charity care.

Those community benefits are difficult to identify and quantify. Various analyses have thus examined not only differences in for-profit and nonprofit hospitals' "outputs," such as uncompensated care and quality of care, but also differences in their operational measures such as cost, profitability, pricing, adoption of technology, and financial policies.

Although those analyses find some differences between for-profit and nonprofit hospitals, in some locations, for some services, they do not reveal consistent patterns.[5] Consequently, analysts and policymakers have reached different conclusions about whether the level of community benefits provided by nonprofit hospitals justifies the tax preferences they receive.

This analysis does not attempt to resolve that issue. Rather, it focuses on only one aspect of the issue: the costs associated with providing the federal tax preferences. And it discusses how much the costs might be reduced if policymakers were to impose a particular type of restriction on hospitals' use of tax-exempt financing.

From the federal taxpayers' perspective, the costs of the tax preferences are the revenues lost from not taxing the income of nonprofit hospitals and the interest income associated with hospital debt. (See Box 1 for a discussion of additional potential costs.) The Joint Committee on Taxation estimates that nonprofit hospitals and their supporting organizations received $2.5 billion in tax savings in 2002 from the income tax exemption and $1.8 billion in tax savings from the preference allowing them to use tax-exempt debt.[6] Taken together, the two tax preferences thus amounted to $4.3 billion in tax savings. Because the estimates do not account for the likely effect of nonprofit hospitals' efforts to minimize their tax burden in response to elimination of the tax preferences, the revenue gain from removing those tax preferences would be smaller than $4.3 billion.[7]

Box 1. Tax Preferences Reduce Nonprofit Hospitals' Cost of Capital

Because of their exemption from income taxation and their ability to use tax- exempt debt, nonprofit hospitals have a significantly lower cost of capital than do for-profit hospitals. In mid-2006, for example, for-profit hospitals had a cost of capital of about 12.9 cents per dollar of investment, while nonprofit hospitals had a cost of capital of only 10.8 cents per dollar of investment. (See Appendix B for a discussion of the cost of capital and the basis for those estimates.) In other words, for-profits would have to receive 12.9 cents each year for each dollar of investment—to cover the original investment and provide a return to investors—while nonprofits would have to receive only 10.8 cents.

The federal tax advantages received by nonprofit hospitals thus lower their cost of capital and national income by as much as 2.1 cents per dollar of investment. The relative contribution of the two tax preferences depends on how nonprofits would finance themselves in the absence of those preferences. One possibility, analyzed in Appendix A, is that nonprofits would use the same level of debt in their projects. Under that assumption, about one-third of the reduction in the cost of capital could be attributed to the ability to use tax-exempt debt; if nonprofit hospitals had to use taxable debt instead, their cost of capital would rise by about 0.65 cents. The remaining two-thirds of the advantage—1.45 cents—would come from the exemption of nonprofit hospitals' income from taxation.

For a discussion of nonprofit hospital financing, see Gerard J. Wedig, Mahmud Hassan, and Michael A. Morrisey, "Tax-Exempt Debt and the Capital Structure of Nonprofit Organizations: An Application to Hospitals," *The Journal of Finance*. vol. 51, no. 4 (1996), pp. 1247-1283.

TAX-EXEMPT BONDS AND TAX ARBITRAGE

State and local governments use tax-exempt bonds to finance their own investments; in addition, they also provide the means for some nongovernmental entities—which can be individuals, private businesses, or nonprofit organizations—to use tax-exempt debt as well. The tax code includes specific provisions designed to limit the tax preference primarily to the financing of investment in operating assets (buildings and equipment). Using low-cost tax-exempt bonds to finance the purchase of higher- yielding taxable securities—tax arbitrage—is prohibited under the tax code and the Department of the Treasury's regulations. Except in limited situations, however, the code does not prevent entities that borrow with tax-exempt bonds from indirectly doing the same thing: earning yields on investment assets not financed with tax- exempt bonds that exceed the interest costs they incur from contemporaneous tax- exempt borrowing.

Nonprofit Hospitals and Tax-Exempt Bonds

New issues of tax-exempt bonds (excluding ones that refinanced previously issued bonds) grew from $103 billion in 1991 to almost $200 billion in 2002, the most recent year for which data are available by type of activity (see Figure 1). That volume includes both governmental bonds and private-activity bonds. Governmental bonds are issued by state and local government entities for public purposes such as the construction of highways, schools, and public hospitals; those bonds averaged 72 percent of new issues over the period. The debt service is usually paid with general tax revenues from state and local taxpayers.

Bonds issued by state and local governments for investments made by private entities generally are classified as private-activity bonds and are taxable. State and local governments and their authorities can, however, issue tax-exempt bonds on behalf of private entities for certain eligible activities, such as the provision of manufacturing structures and equipment, student loans, mortgages for owner-occupied housing, and nonprofit hospital services. The debt service on those private-activity bonds is usually paid with revenues generated by the facilities built with the bond proceeds, not by state and local taxpayers. The amount of tax-exempt private-activity bonds is limited by annual caps on most categories of eligible private-activity bonds but not on tax- exempt bonds issued on behalf of nonprofit hospitals.

State and local governments issued $50 billion in tax-exempt private-activity bonds in 2002. About $10 billion of that amount went to nonprofit hospitals. Over the 199 1- 2002 period, the annual volume of bonds issued on behalf of nonprofit hospitals varied between $4.6 billion (in 1994) and $13.8 billion (in 1998). Those bonds averaged 23 percent of all eligible new issues of private-activity bonds over the period, the largest share for any type of institution using private-activity bonds.

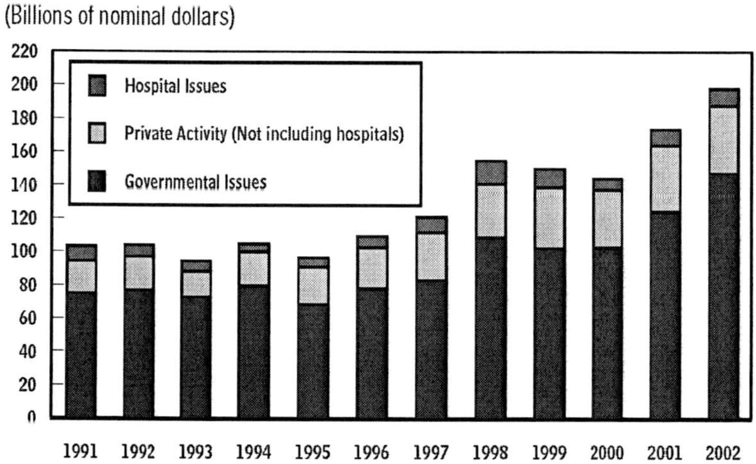

Source: Congressional Budget Office based on data from the Internal Revenue Service drawn from Form 8038 and Form 8038-B information returns.

Note: The figure excludes refunding bonds—those issued to refinance previous borrowing.

Figure 1. The Value of New Tax-Exempt Bonds Issued by Year, 1991 to 2002

Background on Arbitrage Bonds

Purchasers of tax-exempt bonds do not pay income tax on their interest income and therefore are willing to accept a lower interest rate than they can earn on taxable debt of equivalent risk and maturity. That yield differential presents an opportunity for some issuers of tax-exempt debt and a difficult administrative problem for the federal government. Nonprofit organizations (as well as state and local governments) do not pay taxes on their net income, whether that income comes from an operating surplus or their investment earnings. They thus have an incentive to borrow with tax-exempt debt and invest the proceeds in higher-yielding taxable securities. Any higher return on the taxable securities covers the lower interest cost of the tax-exempt debt and, in addition, provides untaxed earnings—or returns from tax arbitrage. That incentive would not exist if the entity using the tax-exempt debt was subject to federal income taxes because the returns from tax arbitrage would be paid to the federal government as income taxes. The tax arbitrage, in effect, provides a transfer from the federal government to the entity engaging in the practice.

To restrict such activity, the tax code specifies that arbitrage bonds are not tax-exempt. Section 148 of the Internal Revenue Code defines an arbitrage bond as:

> Any bond whose proceeds are reasonably expected to be used directly or indirectly (1) to acquire higher-yielding investments or (2) to replace funds which were used directly or indirectly to acquire higher-yielding investments.

The aim is to ensure that bond proceeds are used to increase investment in operating assets (structures and equipment) and are not diverted to the purchase of higher-yielding assets to earn untaxed investment income. The tax code has provisions that prevent the direct diversion of bond proceeds away from investment in physical capital to the earning of investment income. In general, those provisions allow earnings from tax arbitrage only during specified (temporary) periods before the proceeds are needed for the purpose for which the borrowing occurred or on specified types of investments (such as reserve funds). With limited exceptions, any earnings from tax arbitrage must be rebated to the Treasury.[8]

However, the tax code does not prevent all opportunities to borrow at tax-exempt rates while earning higher taxable yields. If an entity's assets are not pledged to pay debt service on its tax-exempt bonds or if the assets have no other direct nexus (connection) to its tax-exempt bonds (within the meaning of the Department of the Treasury's regulations), the arbitrage restrictions do not apply.

For example, consider a nonprofit that has $75 million of investment assets from gifts and accumulated surpluses, all of which is invested in taxable securities earning a return higher than the interest cost of tax-exempt debt. In an economic sense, that institution earns returns from tax arbitrage if it finances $25 million in structures and equipment with tax-exempt bonds rather than internal funds. Although the bond proceeds are being used "directly" to finance the construction of capital facilities, the effect is indistinguishable from using investment assets and replacing those assets with proceeds from private-activity bonds. In effect, by using bonds rather than its own assets to pay for structures and equipment, the institution indirectly uses those bonds to finance higher-yielding investments. The institution gains by the amount by which its earnings on $25 million of securities exceed its interest payments on the bonds.

Treasury regulations include a "replacement proceeds rule" (section 1.148-1(c)) that requires the yield to be restricted on any investment assets or other amounts that have a nexus to a tax-exempt-bond issue that is sufficiently direct for one to conclude that the assets or amounts would have been used to finance the operating assets in the absence of the proceeds from the tax-exempt borrowing. For example, if a hospital pledges securities as collateral for its obligation to repay the debt service on tax- exempt bonds, the securities are treated as replacement proceeds subject to yield restriction under the arbitrage rules. The rules preclude the institution from using its financial assets as collateral for the bonds and then earning a higher rate of return on its assets. The federal government has specific enforcement mechanisms to restrict bond issuers' yields on their investment assets so that the return on the investment assets is not materially higher than the interest cost on the tax-exempt bonds (see Box 2).

As discussed, the replacement proceeds rule applies when there is a sufficient connection between certain of the entity's assets and the tax-exempt bonds, as when an entity pledges assets in payment for the debt service. The rule is intended to address indirect arrangements that provide tax arbitrage, but administering the rule is difficult in practice. It is arguably ineffective because accounting reports typically do not reveal such relationships. Moreover, the need to establish a direct connection (such as a pledge) between investment assets and debt service is inconsistent with typical practices in bond markets, as bond-rating agencies base credit ratings on institutions' overall investment assets and cash on hand because those assets and their earnings can ultimately be used to pay for debt service or can be used to cover expenses to free up other funds to pay for debt service.

BOX 2. HOW THE TREASURY DEPARTMENT RESTRICTS THE YIELDS ON INVESTMENT ASSETS

The Treasury restricts the yields on investment assets using two mechanisms. In the first, the borrowers' investment portfolio is left undisturbed, but the borrower is required to rebate to the federal government the excess yields earned on assets equal in amount to the bond proceeds. In the second, the borrower is required to sell an amount of assets equal to the value of the bonds and invest the sale proceeds in a specially created Treasury debt instrument (State and Local Government Series). Those Treasury bonds, called SLUGS, are designed to provide a yield that offsets the interest cost on the tax-exempt bonds.

That attribute of the tax code is not unique to nonprofit hospitals. It applies equally to other nonprofit institutions such as colleges and universities, which have sizable financial assets invested in financial securities. Nor does the feature necessarily constitute a "loophole." The current tax arbitrage rules do ensure that a bond issue is associated with the acquisition of new capital, and they do reduce its cost. Nonetheless, a change in the rules that would broaden the definition of tax arbitrage—identifying it on the basis of institutions' investment assets instead of relying on establishing a direct connection between bond proceeds and higher-yielding investments—would serve to decrease the tax benefits going to nonprofit hospitals should policymakers decide to reduce them.[9]

ESTIMATING ISSUES

Estimating nonprofit hospitals' prior and future use of tax-exempt bonds as tax arbitrage under a broad definition is a complicated procedure. This section discusses the economic concepts and data issues employed in making those estimates.

Nonprofit hospitals often borrow using tax-exempt bonds to finance capital investments even though they hold substantial assets that they could sell to pay for new facilities. CBO's analysis looked at every hospital that had tax-exempt debt on its balance sheet in 2002 and at every hospital for which tax-exempt debt was issued in 2002 and asked how much of the hospital's outstanding bond issues or new bond issue could have been replaced with existing investment assets. If the hospital's assets exceeded its outstanding bonds or its new bond issue, the analysis considered those bonds to be arbitrage bonds since the hospital presumably chose to use bonds because the investment assets would earn a greater return than the interest paid on the bonds. If the hospital's outstanding bond issues or new bond issue exceeded its investment assets, only that portion of the bonds that could have been replaced by assets would qualify as arbitrage.

Data Issues

To estimate nonprofit hospitals' use of arbitrage bonds, CBO used data from two different sources, and, for one of those sources, two different versions.

Every nonprofit hospital must annually file a Form 990 information return with the IRS detailing its revenues, expenses, assets, and liabilities. The IRS makes available a stratified sample of those returns, which CBO used to estimate the investment assets and outstanding stock of tax-exempt bonds for nonprofit hospitals that had borrowed in 2002 using tax-exempt debt.

Every state and local government and other authority that issues tax-exempt bonds must file a Form 8038 information return with the IRS that details a bond issue's dollar value and purpose, as well as other financial information. CBO used the Form 8038 returns to estimate the volume of nonprofit hospitals' tax-exempt borrowing in 2002. Returns were filed for 384 bond issues, of which 310 were new and 74 were refinancing previously issued bonds. According to the returns, the 310 new issues were on behalf of 434 entities.

A few returns came from state or local authorities that issued bonds and divided the proceeds among multiple hospitals that were not identified on the Form 8038 returns. More frequently, returns listed multiple entities without specifying the share of bond proceeds each received. By contacting issuing authorities, parent organizations, and hospitals, CBO identified 348 hospitals that, in fact, received bond proceeds. Of those hospitals, CBO dropped 38 from the data set because of accounting complications between parent and subsidiary hospitals or because they could not be matched with a Form 990 information return. Those adjustments left 310 nonprofit hospitals available for the analysis; they received nearly 90 percent—$8.4 billion of $9.5 billion—of proceeds from new bond issues reported on the Form 8038 returns for 2002.

To determine how much of the outstanding stock of bonds could be considered to earn returns from tax arbitrage under a broader definition and to estimate the effect that broader definition might have on new bond issues, CBO combined information on investment assets and the outstanding stock of tax-exempt debt from the IRS Form 990 with the bond issuance data from the Form 8038.[10] Because the IRS Form 990 data are based on a sample of hospitals and therefore often failed to match some of the Form 8038 returns, CBO supplemented the IRS information with data maintained by the National Center for Charitable Statistics at the Urban Institute, which includes virtually all Form 990 information returns filed by nonprofit organizations.[11]

Measuring Nonprofit Hospitals' Use of Arbitrage Bonds

Several conceptual and measurement issues arise in determining how much of the outstanding stock of tax-exempt debt and the new tax-exempt borrowing would be classified as earning returns from tax arbitrage under the broader definition.

Measuring Arbitrage Bonds

CBO estimated the outstanding stock of bonds that were earning returns from tax arbitrage under the broader measure by comparing a hospital's investment assets net of accumulated depreciation with its outstanding stock of tax-exempt bonds.[12] If investment assets exceeded the outstanding stock of bonds, all of the bonds were deemed to be arbitrage bonds. If the stock of bonds exceeded investment assets, then the level of arbitrage bonds was considered to equal the investment assets. Under that measure, a nonprofit hospital's arbitrage bonds were thus the lesser of the outstanding stock of bonds or the investment assets.

CBO refers to that measurement approach as the "historical measure" because it is based primarily on the outstanding stock of tax-exempt debt, which reflects the history of all bond issues that have not been completely retired (paid off). All of the data for that measure of arbitrage bonds come from the Form 990 information returns.

Implementing a broader definition of tax arbitrage, however, would of course be forward-looking. It would not look back to past issues and require a rebate of tax arbitrage returns earned on those bonds that could have been replaced with financing from investment assets. Instead, a nonprofit hospital's new bonds would be compared to its investment assets. If investment assets exceeded the dollar value of the new bond issue, all the bonds would be considered to be earning returns from tax arbitrage. If the new bond issue exceeded investment assets, arbitrage bonds would equal the investment assets, and some of the bond issue would not be considered to be earning returns from tax arbitrage. Thus, arbitrage bonds would be the lesser of the bond issue or the investment assets. In the early years of implementation of such a policy, a relatively large share of new issues would probably be judged to be arbitrage bonds because a large amount of investment assets would be available in comparison with the size of any one year's new issues.

CBO refers to that measurement approach as the "first-year measure" because it measures the immediate effect of broadening the definition of tax arbitrage. The first-year measure uses data on investment assets from the Form 990 information returns and data on annual bond issues from the Form 8038 information returns.

As the years progressed and a larger share of investment assets would have their yield restricted to cover prior years' new issues, fewer new issues would be classified as arbitrage bonds. Under an assumption that hospitals would not alter their accumulation of assets or their tax-exempt borrowing in response to the change in definition, the existing balance between the stock of investment assets and the outstanding stock of tax-exempt bonds could be viewed as a possible equilibrium. Therefore, if a new bond issue was less than the difference between the investment assets and the outstanding stock of tax-exempt bonds (that difference being the relationship observed in the historical measure), the level of arbitrage bonds would be equal to the new issue. If a new bond issue was greater than that difference, the level of arbitrage bonds would be equal to the difference. Thus, the level of arbitrage bonds would be the lesser of the new issue of tax-exempt bonds or the difference between the investment assets and the outstanding stock of tax-exempt bonds. In essence, the measure assumes that the historical measure of arbitrage bonds has already been applied and that new bond issues are measured against any residual assets not applied to previously issued bonds.

CBO refers to that measurement approach as the "steady-state measure" because it measures the effect of the change in definition when it is fully phased in. It uses data on investment assets and the outstanding stock of tax-exempt bonds from the Form 990 information returns and data on annual bond issues from the Form 8038 information returns.

Measuring Investment Assets

For all hospitals (on the basis of the sample of Form 990 information returns weighted to produce population estimates) and those that borrowed in 2002 (on the basis of the match of the data from the Forms 990 and 8038), net investment assets exceeded the outstanding stock of tax-exempt debt (see Table 1). Also, the hospitals borrowing in 2002 had, on average, larger outstanding stocks of bonds than did all hospitals, because the set of 2002 borrowers excluded all hospitals that never borrowed: the medians were $10.5 million and zero, respectively. Both of those medians are underestimates that reflect misreporting of part of the taxexempt-bond stock as mortgages on the Form 990 (an issue discussed below).

Table 1. Summary of Data Used to Estimate Nonprofit Hospitals' Level of Arbitrage Bonds, 2002 (Millions of dollars)

	All Hospitals		Hospitals That Borrowed in 2002	
	Total	Median	Total	Media n
Number of Hospitals	2,912	n.a.	310	n.a.
Net Investment Assets	105,548	3.55	21,188	14.83
Outstanding Stock of Tax-Exempt Debt	93,655	0	17,902	10.53
Mortgage Debt	31,304	1.04	4,163	0.92
Adjusted Outstanding Stock of Tax-Exempt Debt[a]	123,844	10.00	21,851	23.36
New Bond Issues	n.a.	n.a.	8,384	15.05

Source: Congressional Budget Office based on data from the Internal Revenue Service drawn from Form 8038 and Form 990 information returns.

Note: n.a. = not applicable.

a. The adjusted outstanding stock of tax-exempt debt includes most mortgages reported on Form 990 added to the stock of tax-exempt bonds.

Hospitals accumulate investment assets for a variety of reasons, including to earn income, to protect against uncertainty (precautionary savings), to enhance their reputation, and to honor gift restrictions. Some of those reasons might imply that some investment assets should not to be counted when estimating arbitrage bonds.

The need to hold some level of precautionary savings is the most compelling reason that, even with a concern about tax arbitrage, it may be appropriate for nonprofits to hold some investment assets that are not subject to yield restriction. Those precautionary savings may be valuable to the hospital and its ability to provide community benefits. The bond-rating agencies offer higher credit ratings as a hospital's days of cash on hand increases, and financial markets translate those higher ratings into lower interest rates.[13] Nonprofit hospitals' precautionary savings are, in fact, substantial: the median number of days of cash on hand for the 310 nonprofit hospitals that issued tax-exempt debt in 2002 was 117 days and ranged from a high exceeding 38,000 days to a low of zero.

The broadened definition of arbitrage probably could be implemented without violating gift restrictions imposed on some investment assets. For example, a $1 million gift to finance a cancer center would not be violated by restricting the yield on it in order to issue tax-exempt debt to purchase a magnetic resonance imaging machine (MRI). The gift would not be spent on the MRI; only the earnings of the gift would be affected. Furthermore, not including such gifts in the calculation of tax arbitrage would create an incentive for hospital managers to ask donors to impose restrictions on their gifts so the hospitals could earn tax arbitrage profits. That response might substantially reduce hospitals' ability to use such gifts to provide community benefits: restrictions on gifts increase the share of benefits appropriable to the donor while simultaneously decreasing the expected value of the community benefits the hospital can generate with the gifts.

Measuring Tax-Exempt Debt

One difficulty with the data is that tax-exempt borrowing may be misreported. When the National Council of Health Facilities Finance Authorities compared the Form 990 returns, including supporting statements, and the audited financial statements in two states for all hospitals that appeared in CBO's Form 8038 data set, that analysis revealed that substantial tax-exempt debt was reported on the Form 990 returns as mortgages.

As a result, CBO examined the Form 990 returns and supporting statements filed by a portion of the 310 hospitals that borrowed in 2002. In every instance in which the hospital reported zero tax-exempt liabilities and positive mortgage liabilities, those mortgage liabilities were almost entirely (99.6 percent) tax-exempt liabilities. In many cases, a parent corporation borrowed using tax-exempt debt and made a loan to the hospital, which the hospital did not report as a tax-exempt liability. In instances when hospitals reported both tax-exempt liabilities and mortgages, 84 percent of the mortgage liabilities were tax-exempt liabilities.

CBO used those percentages to reclassify mortgage liabilities reported on the Form 990 returns as tax-exempt liabilities (see Table 1). Before that reclassification, the median outstanding stock of tax-exempt debt was zero; at least half of all of the nonprofit hospitals did not appear to take advantage of that tax preference. After mortgages were added to that stock of debt, the median rose to $10 million. Making the adjustment increased the outstanding stock of tax-exempt bonds for all nonprofit hospitals (based on the IRS sample of Form 990 information returns) by 32 percent, from $93.7 billion to $123.8 billion. The outstanding stock of tax-exempt bonds for the 310 hospitals in the Form 8038 data set (using the Urban Institute's Form 990 data set for the stock of bonds) increased 22 percent, from $17.9 billion to $21.9 billion.

ARBITRAGE BOND ESTIMATES

As explained, the data used to estimate the level of arbitrage bonds under a broader definition of tax arbitrage included information on 310 of the 348 nonprofit hospitals that borrowed using tax-exempt debt in 2002. If those 310 hospitals' investment assets and outstanding stock of tax-exempt debt were typical, the estimates for future groups of hospital borrowers would probably be similar. To evaluate that assumption would require examining additional years of Form 8038 data, but a comparison of all nonprofit hospitals in 1996 and 2002 shows that the historical measure of tax arbitrage was similar in the two years (see Appendix A).

Nonprofit hospitals borrow with tax-exempt debt at the same time that they earn a higher rate of return on investment assets. If the broader definition of tax arbitrage is applied to the stocks of accumulated assets and tax-exempt debt that those 310 hospitals reported in 2002 (that is, the historical measure), 57 percent of the hospitals were earning returns from tax arbitrage on almost $11 billion of tax-exempt debt, or 61 percent of their outstanding stock of bonds (see the historical measure in Table 2).[14]

Table 2. The Level of Arbitrage by Nonprofit Hospitals That Borrowed in 2002, without Adjustments to Correct for Misreporting

	Historical Measure[a]		First-Year Measure[b]		Steady-State Measure[c]	
	Number	Percentage	Number	Percentage	Number	Percentage
	Number of Hospitals with Tax-Exempt Debt					
Hospitals Conducting						
Arbitrage Under a Broader Definition	178	57.4	264	85.2	163	52.6
Full	77	24.8	156	50.3	86	27.7
Partial	101	32.6	108	34.8	77	24.8
Hospitals Not						
Conducting Arbitrage	132	42.6	46	14.8	147	47.4
	Value of Tax-Exempt Debt (Millions of dollars)					
Arbitrage Under a Broader Definition	10,896	60.9	5,385	64.2	2,899	34.6
Full	5,752	32.1	4,032	48.1	1,716	20.5
Partial	5,143	28.7	1,353	16.1	1,183	14.1
Debt Not						
Deemed Arbitrage	7,007	39.1	2,999	35.8	5,484	65.4
Total	**17,902**	**100.0**	**8,384**	**100.0**	**8,384**	**100.0**

Source: Congressional Budget Office based on data from the Internal Revenue Service drawn from Form 8038 and Form 990 information returns.

Note: Calculations are based on information on 310 hospitals.

a. The historical measure is based on the hospitals' outstanding stock of tax-exempt bonds and does not include bonds issued in 2002.

b. The first-year measure, based on bonds issued in 2002, estimates what the initial effects of implementing a broader definition of tax arbitrage would be.

c. The steady-state measure, based on the bonds issued in 2002, estimates what the effects would be after the hospitals have adjusted to the initial implementation of a broader definition of tax arbitrage.

Table 3. The Level of Arbitrage by Nonprofit Hospitals That Borrowed in 2002, as Adjusted to Correct for Misreporting

	Historical Measure[a]		First-Year Measure[b]		Steady-State Measure[c]	
	Number	Percentage	Number	Percentage	Number	Percentage
	Number of Hospitals with Tax-Exempt Debt					
Hospitals Conducting						
Arbitrage Under a Broader Definition	249	80.3	264	85.2	116	37.4
Full	101	32.6	156	50.3	57	18.4
Partial	148	47.7	108	34.8	59	19.0
Hospitals Not						
Conducting Arbitrage	61	19.7	46	14.8	194	62.6
	Value of Tax-Exempt Debt (Millions of dollars)					
Arbitrage Under a Broader Definition	13,171	60.3	5,385	64.2	2,360	28.2
Full	6,665	30.5	4,032	48.1	1,217	14.5
Partial	6,506	29.8	1,353	16.1	1,143	13.6
Debt Not						
Deemed Arbitrage	8,680	39.7	2,999	35.8	6,024	71.8
Total	**21,851**	**100.0**	**8,384**	**100.0**	**8,384**	**100.0**

Source: Congressional Budget Office based on data from the Internal Revenue Service drawn from Form 8038 and Form 990 information returns.

Notes: The estimates in this table incorporate CBO's adjustments to the figures for hospitals' outstanding stock of tax-exempt bonds to correct for their misreporting of mortgages as taxable liabilities.

Calculations are based on information on 310 hospitals.

a. The historical measure is based on the hospitals' outstanding stock of tax-exempt bonds and does not include bonds issued in 2002.

b. The first-year measure, based on bonds issued in 2002, estimates what the initial effects of implementing a broader definition of tax arbitrage would be.

c. The steady-state measure, based on the bonds issued in 2002, estimates what the effects would be after the hospitals have adjusted to the initial implementation of a broader definition of tax arbitrage.

Table 4. The Level of Arbitrage by Nonprofit Hospitals That Borrowed in 2002, as Adjusted to Correct for Misreporting and to Allow for Precautionary Savings

	Historical Measure[a]		First-Year Measure[b]		Steady-State Measure[c]	
	Number	Percentage	Number	Percentage	Number	Percentage
	Number of Hospitals with Tax-Exempt Debt					
Hospitals Conducting						
Arbitrage Under a Broader Definition	109	35.2	116	37.4	47	15.2
Full	40	12.9	68	21.9	22	7.1
Partial	69	22.3	48	15.5	25	8.1
Hospitals Not						
Conducting Arbitrage	201	64.8	194	62.6	263	84.8
	Value of Tax-Exempt Debt (Millions of dollars)					
Arbitrage Under a Broader Definition	7,218	33.0	2,716	32.4	761	9.1
Full	3,068	14.0	1,629	19.4	363	4.3
Partial	4,150	19.0	1,087	13.0	398	4.7
Debt Not						
Deemed Arbitrage	14,633	67.0	5,668	67.6	7,623	90.9
Total	**21,851**	**100.0**	**8,384**	**100.0**	**8,384**	**100.0**

Source: Congressional Budget Office based on data from the Internal Revenue Service drawn from Form 8038 and Form 990 information returns.

Notes: The estimates in this table incorporate CBO's adjustments to the figures for hospitals' outstanding stock of tax-exempt bonds to correct for their misreporting of mortgages as taxable liabilities. The estimates also allow for hospitals to maintain 100 days of precautionary savings that is not subject to yield restriction.

Calculations are based on information on 310 hospitals.

a. The historical measure is based on the hospitals' outstanding stock of tax-exempt bonds and does not include bonds issued in 2002.

b. The first-year measure, based on bonds issued in 2002, estimates what the initial effects of implementing a broader definition of tax arbitrage would be.

c. The steady-state measure, based on the bonds issued in 2002, estimates what the effects would be after the hospitals have adjusted to the initial implementation of a broader definition of tax arbitrage.

However, that stock of tax-exempt debt is underestimated because it does not include mortgages misreported as taxable liabilities. When the stock of tax-exempt bonds is corrected, 80 percent of that population of nonprofit hospitals were earning returns on tax arbitrage on almost $13 billion of tax-exempt debt, or 60 percent of their outstanding stock of bonds (see the historical measure in Table 3).[15]

Those estimates are sensitive to the amount of investment assets allowed to escape yield restriction for precautionary savings. If that allowance is set to 100 days of operating expenses, 35 percent of those nonprofit hospitals were earning returns on tax arbitrage on an outstanding stock of bonds equal to $7.2 billion, or 33 percent of their outstanding stock (see the historical measure in Table 4).

Under an assumption that the current relationship between hospitals' accumulation of investment assets and tax-exempt borrowing is not affected by the broader definition of tax arbitrage, at some point in the future the share of new bond issues classified as arbitrage bonds would reach a steady state and be substantially less than the previous estimates. Absent an allowance for precautionary savings, about 37 percent of all hos pitals borrowing with tax-exempt debt in 2002 would be earning tax arbitrage on about $2.4 billion, or 28 percent, of their bonds (see the steady-state measure in Table 3). If allowance is made for 100 days of precautionary savings, those numbers would decline to 15 percent of hospitals earning arbitrage returns on about $761 million, or 9 percent of their bonds (see the steady-state measure in Table 4).

Over time, the federal government's net fiscal condition from a broadened definition of tax arbitrage would improve. Hospitals would have to reduce their new issues of tax-exempt bonds (either reducing investment in operating assets or switching to taxable debt) by 28 percent (or by 9 percent if the policy accommodated precautionary savings). For example, if tax-exempt bonds provide an annual benefit of $1.8 billion to nonprofit hospitals, as estimated for 2002, then over time the broadened definition of tax arbitrage would save $504 million per year (or $162 million if allowance was made for precautionary savings). If hospitals chose instead to subject their investment assets to yield restriction, tax expenditures would not change but the government would realize an equivalent amount in reduced borrowing costs or increased earnings.[16]

Those estimates of tax arbitrage reflect a variety of judgments about how best to measure the stock of tax-exempt debt, how many investment assets to hold aside for precautionary savings, and which measurement best represents the effect of the changed definition of tax arbitrage. The remainder of this section describes how those judgments affect the number of hospitals using arbitrage bonds and the share of bonds classified as arbitrage bonds.

Estimates with Hospitals' Bond Stock Unadjusted

With no adjustments to the outstanding stock of tax-exempt debt or allowance for precautionary savings, the 310 hospitals borrowing in 2002 had $17.9 billion in outstanding bonds (see the historical measure in Table 2). As described, the historical measure indicates that 57 percent of the hospitals used arbitrage bonds and that 61 percent ($10.9 billion) of their outstanding stock of bonds was earning returns from tax arbitrage.[17]

In the first year following a broadening of the definition of tax arbitrage, 85 percent of the 310 hospitals borrowing with tax-exempt funds in 2002 would have arbitrage bonds, and 64 percent of their $8.4 billion bond volume ($5.4 billion) would be considered arbitrage bonds (see the first-year measure in Table 2).

The steady-state measure of arbitrage bonds is calculated once a balance has been established between asset accumulation and bond issuance. About 53 percent of hospitals would have arbitrage bonds and 35 percent of their $8.4 billion in new issues ($2.9 billion) would be arbitrage bonds (see the steady-state measure in Table 2).

Estimates with Bond Stock Adjusted

Adjusting the outstanding stock of tax-exempt debt to include the tax-exempt bonds classified as mortgage liabilities on the Form 990 information returns increases the outstanding stock of bonds and the share of those bonds classified as arbitrage bonds under the broader measure (see Table 3). For the historical measure, the share of hospitals that earned returns from tax arbitrage rises to 80 percent. Although the increased stock of tax-exempt debt increases the dollar value of arbitrage bonds, the share of bonds classified as arbitrage bonds is reduced slightly, to 60 percent (from a share of 61 percent using unadjusted bond data).

The percentage of hospitals earning returns from tax arbitrage and the dollar volume of new issues classified as arbitrage bonds in the first year following the implementation of the broader definition of tax arbitrage do not change from the estimates relying on unadjusted bond data because the first-year measure does not use the stock of tax-exempt debt in calculating the level of arbitrage bonds. In the steady state, though, the share of hospitals with arbitrage bonds is reduced to 37 percent, and the share of new bond issues classified as arbitrage bonds declines to 28 percent ($2.4 billion).

Adjustment for Precautionary Savings

If investment assets are reduced by precautionary savings adequate to finance 100 days of operating expenses, the percentage of hospitals earning tax arbitrage returns and the share of bonds classified as arbitrage bonds are reduced for all three measures. In the steady state, only 15 percent of hospitals use arbitrage bonds, and only 9 percent of the bond volume, $761 million, is classified as arbitrage bonds (see Table 4). [18]

To summarize (as done in Figure 2), first, the share of the stock of tax-exempt bonds classified as arbitrage bonds (the historical measure) exceeds the share of new issues classified as arbitrage bonds once an equilibrium between asset accumulation and tax- exempt borrowing (the steady-state measure) is established. Second, the adjustment of the tax-exempt-bond stock to include bonds misreported as mortgages decreases slightly the share of arbitrage bonds. Third, setting aside larger amounts of investment assets as precautionary savings decreases the share of arbitrage bonds.

Hospitals' Response to Implementation of a Broader Arbitrage Definition

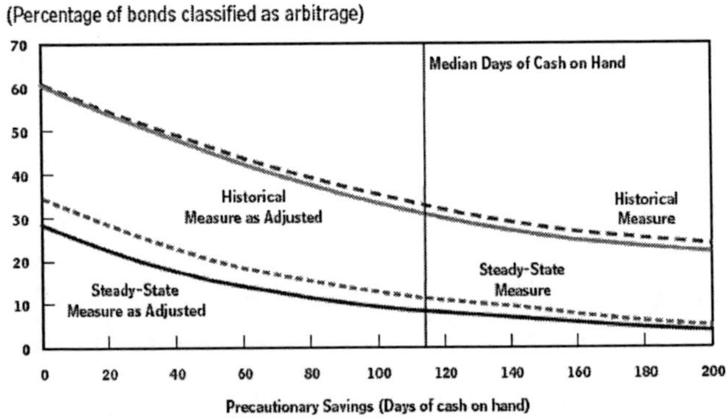

Source: Congressional Budget Office based on data from the Internal Revenue Service (IRS).

Notes: For both the historical and steady-state measures, the unadjusted estimates are based on hospitals' outstanding stock of tax-exempt debt as reported on IRS Form 990, and the adjusted estimates are based on that stock as corrected to include mortgages financed with tax-exempt debt.

The median number of days of cash on hand for the 310 nonprofit hospitals in 2002 was 117. The average number of days of cash on hand for for-profit hospitals in 2003 was 135.

Figure 2. Nonprofit Hospitals' Arbitrage Bonds and Precautionary Savings, 2002

Nonprofit hospitals would probably change their behavior in response to a broadened definition of tax arbitrage. Those institutions with large enough portfolios would see an effective increase in the cost of capital. The decrease in tax benefits and the increase in their cost of capital would lead them to reduce their investment in structures and equipment. That change in behavior would have several implications.

First, the hospitals would borrow less so the actual quantity of tax arbitrage bonds under the expanded definition would be smaller than implied by the steady-state figures calculated here. As with any tax increase, the volume of the activity being taxed tends to decrease in consequence.

Second, broadening the rule would result in two different costs of capital for nonprofit hospitals. Nonprofits with larger portfolios of investment assets would be more likely to be subject to the rule and thus effectively face higher interest costs associated with financing using taxable debt. Hospitals with smaller amounts of such assets would be more likely to continue to receive the benefit of tax-exempt financing. Both would still face lower costs of capital than for-profit hospitals. But the different borrowing costs of the two groups of nonprofit hospitals could engender inefficiencies by creating a new differential in capital costs.

The ultimate outcome for efficient allocation of resources would be uncertain, depending on which dominated, the potentially efficiency-enhancing effect of narrowing the cost-of-capital differential between nonprofit and for-profit hospitals, or the potentially efficiency-damaging effect of creating a capital-cost differential among nonprofit hospitals, depending on their portfolios of investment assets.

APPENDIX A: A PREVIOUS ESTIMATE OF NONPROFIT HOSPITALS' USE OF ARBITRAGE BONDS

Aprevious effort, by William Gentry, to estimate nonprofit hospitals' use of arbitrage bonds employed Form 990 information returns from 1996 to compare investment assets to the outstanding stock of tax-exempt bonds, the Congressional Budget Office's (CBO's) historical measure.[19] In comparison, in the information from 2002 that CBO used, the total number of hospitals was higher by about 20 percent and the outstanding stock of tax-exempt bonds by almost 80 percent (see Table A-1). But in both analyses, the percentage of hospitals with arbitrage bonds (about 90 percent) and the percentage of tax-exempt-bond volume satisfying the broader definition of tax arbitrage (about 58 percent) were very similar. Nonprofit hospitals' behavior does not seem to have changed much over the 1996-2002 period. The relationship between hospitals' accumulation of investment assets and use of tax-exempt debt appears to have been stable.

Table A-1. Comparison of CBO's Estimates and Earlier Estimates of Nonprofit Hospitals' Use of Arbitrage Bonds

	CBO's Estimates (2002)[a]		Gentry's Estimates (1996)	
	Number	Percentage	Number	Percent age
	Number of Hospitals with Tax-Exempt Debt			
Hospitals Conducting Arbitrage				
Under a Broader Definition	1,149	90.1	918	88.0
Full	395	31.0	374	35.9
Partial	754	59.1	544	52.2
Hospitals Not				
Conducting Arbitrage	127	9.9	125	12.0
Total	**1,276**	**100.0**	**1,043**	**100.0**
	Value of Tax-Exempt Debt (Millions of dollars)			
Any Arbitrage	54,136	57.8	32,600	58.3
Full arbitrage	30,857	32.9	19,500	34.9
Partial arbitrage (Includes only arbitrage portion)	23,279	24.9	13,100	23.4
No Arbitrage (Includes nonarbitrage portion of partial arbitrage bonds)	39,518	42.2	23,300	41.7
Total	**93,655**	**100.0**	**55,900**	**100.0**

Source: Congressional Budget Office (CBO) based on data from the Internal Revenue Service drawn from information returns Form 990; William M. Gentry, "Debt Investment and Endowment Accumulation: The Case of Not-for-Profit Hospitals," *Journal of Health Economics*, vol. 21, no. 5 (2002), pp. 845-872.

a. The estimates by CBO presented here convey its "historical measure," which is based on the hospitals' outstanding stock of tax-exempt bonds and does not include bonds issued in 2002.

APPENDIX B: THE COST OF CAPITAL

Potential Economic Costs from Nonprofit Hospitals' Tax Preferences

The tax preferences provided to nonprofit hospitals might distort investment choices and reduce national income if they cause investment capital to move from higher- return projects that are subject to taxation to lower-return projects that are exempt. The first step in estimating the potential magnitude of such costs is to estimate the difference in the cost of capital between for-profit and nonprofit hospitals.

The Congressional Budget Office estimates that the cost of capital for a for-profit hospital was about 12.9 cents per dollar of investment in June 2006 (see Table B-1). In other words, investors would have been willing to invest in a for-profit hospital only if they expected to earn at least 12.9 cents each year for each dollar of investment. In contrast, a nonprofit hospital that could use tax-exempt debt had a cost of capital of about 10.8 cents per dollar, about 2.1 cents per dollar less than a for-profit hospital.[20] Roughly one-third of that reduction in the cost of capital comes from the use of tax- exempt bonds if taxable debt is substituted for tax-exempt debt. The balance results from the nonprofit hospitals' exemption from corporate income taxes.

The reduction in a nonprofit hospital's cost of capital provides an equivalent reduction in the pretax real return that it requires. In mid-2006, for-profit hospitals needed to obtain a return of at least 7.7 percent (their cost of capital minus economic depreciation) to make capital investments economically worthwhile. Because tax savings reduce nonprofits' cost of capital, they can earn a lower return on investment than their for-profit counterparts: 5.6 percent. That lower required pretax return gives nonprofit hospitals an incentive to pursue additional projects that make sense only because of the tax exemption. A project that returns 6 percent, for example, could be pursued by a nonprofit hospital but not by a for-profit hospital. But the only way to finance that project is to take capital away from an unsubsidized investment that would earn at least 7.7 percent.

If nonprofit hospitals invest in lower-value activities because of that lower pretax return, those investments contribute less to national income—between almost zero and 2 cents per dollar of investment—than unsubsidized investments returning 7.7 cents per dollar do.

Table B-1. Scenarios Illustrating the Cost of Capital for For-Profit and Nonprofit Hospitals

	For-Profit Hospital	Nonprofit Hospital	
		Scenario 1	Scenario 2
Assumed Mix of Financing (Percent)			
Debt, and its tax status	38, taxable	38, tax-exempt	38, taxable
Equity[a]	62	62	62
Cost of Capital (Cents per dollar)	12.89	10.79	11.44
Decrease in Nonprofit Hospital's Cost			
Relative to For-Profit Hospital's Cost			
Cents per dollar	n.a.	2.10	1.45
Percent	n.a.	16.3	11.2
Tax Preferences' Contributions to Decrease in Cost of Capital (Percent)			
Income tax exemption	n.a.	69	100
Tax-exempt bonds	n.a.	31	0

Source: Congressional Budget Office.

a. Equity financing is based on a hospital's endowment funds.

The Derivation of the Cost of Capital and the Pretax Real Return

A firm's cost of capital depends on many factors: the interest rate on debt financing, the return paid to those who provide equity financing, the rate at which the productive life of assets declines (economic depreciation), the tax treatment of each of those factors, and the corporate income tax rate. The exemption from income taxes eliminates a nonprofit hospital's expenses from that source, and the exclusion of interest income on its debt from federal taxation lowers the interest rate on its debt financing.

The cost of capital per dollar of investment, c, is equal to

$$c = (R+d)(1-uz) / (1-u)$$

where

R is the organization's real after-tax discount rate, a weighted average of the pretax real returns for the three potential financing sources (taxable debt, tax-exempt debt, and equity), with taxable debt adjusted for its deductibility;

d is the rate at which the economic value of the asset depreciates;

u is the corporate tax rate; and

z is the present value of tax depreciation per dollar of investment

R depends on the type of financing used by the hospital. For example, a for-profit hospital financing an investment with taxable debt would have to pay lenders, on the basis of the Baa bond rates that prevailed in June 2006, about 6.9 percent in nominal terms. But the corporation can deduct that interest expense, so the after-tax interest rate would be 4.5 percent. With expected economywide inflation of 1.8 percent deducted, the hospital would pay a real after-tax interest rate of 2.7 percent.[21] The hospital would pay a 7.0 percent real return to finance the investment with equity, a cost that is not deductible.[22] Since most hospitals finance an investment with a mixture of debt and equity, the real after-tax discount rate would be a weighted average of 2.7 percent for debt and 7.0 percent for equity.

To that discount rate must be added economic depreciation. That sum is adjusted for the value of tax-depreciation allowances (to account for the excess of tax-depreciation allowances compared to economic depreciation), and the result is then increased to reflect the income taxes paid on net income. The result is the firm's cost of capital.

A nonprofit hospital can borrow at a lower interest rate, about 5.15 percent rather than 6.9 percent, because its debt is tax-exempt. The difference in interest rates is determined by the marginal tax rate (25 percent in this example) of the bond purchaser to whom the bond issuer must sell the last bond. However, the nonprofit hospital cannot deduct that interest expense (because it pays no income taxes). After an adjustment for 1.8 percent inflation, the real interest rate is 3.35 percent. The hospital would pay a 7.0 percent real return on any portion of the investment financed with equity (the opportunity cost of not investing its assets). If the hospital finances with a mixture of tax-exempt debt and equity, the real discount rate would be a weighted average of 3.35 percent for debt and 7 percent for equity. That rate is adjusted upward for economic depreciation, but adjustments for tax depreciation and income tax payments are not necessary because the nonprofit pays no federal income taxes.

The pretax real return, r, that must be earned to make the investment economically worthwhile for the hospital is:

$$r = c - d$$

that is, the cost of capital minus economic depreciation.

End Notes

[1] Nonprofit hospitals also benefit from the fact that donors' charitable contributions to them are tax-deductible and from several state and local tax preferences.

[2] The revenues that the federal government would gain from eliminating those tax advantages would be lower than $4.3 billion because nonprofit hospitals would adjust their behavior to minimize their tax burden.

[3] The terms "debt" and "bonds" are used interchangeably to refer to debt with maturities in excess of a year. The dollar figures for such debt cited in this analysis also include any leasing arrangements that are tax-exempt.

[4] Internal Revenue Service, 1969. Revenue Ruling 69-545, 1969-2 C.B. 117, available at www.irs.gov/pub/irs-tege/rr69-545.pdf.

[5] See Congressional Budget Office, *Nonprofit Hospitals and the Provision of Community Benefits* (December 2006). See also Frank A. Sloan, "Not-for-Profit Ownership and Hospital Behavior," in A.J. Culyer and J.P. Newhouse, eds., *Handbook of Health Economics*, eds., vol. 1 (Amsterdam: Elsevier Science B.V., 2000), pp. 1142-1174; and Frank Schlesinger and Bradford H. Gray, "How Nonprofits Matter in American Medicine, and What to Do About It," *Health Affairs*, vol. 25, no. 4 (2006), pp. 287-303.

[6] Memorandum from Thomas A. Barthold, Joint Committee on Taxation, to James Baumgardner and G. Thomas Woodward, Congressional Budget Office, September 12, 2006.
Supporting organizations are entities formed specifically to provide financial support for a hospital classified under the Internal Revenue Code as a 501(c)(3)—nonprofit—organization. In addition, JCT estimates that, in 2002, nonprofit hospitals received these benefits from tax preferences: $1.8 billion from the deductibility of charitable contributions on federal income taxes, $0.5 billion from their exemption from state corporate income taxes, $2.8 billion from their exemption from state sales taxes, and $3.1 billion from their exemption from state and local property taxes—bringing the total tax benefits to $12.6 billion.

[7] Absent the incentive to maximize profits that is provided by owners expecting a return on their investment, a nonprofit organization might reduce its net income (and its tax base) substantially by lowering its prices, shifting costs from related for-profit entities, or increasing compensation to employees. Those responses are discussed in Congressional Budget Office, *Taxing the Untaxed Business Sector* (July 2005).

[8] Generally, a rebate is not required if all of the proceeds are spent for the purpose of the borrowing within certain prescribed time periods. The rebate requirement also does not apply to small general purpose governmental units, usually defined as entities that issue no more than $5 million of tax-exempt governmental bonds in a year.

[9] Alternatively, a limit on a nonprofit hospital's outstanding stock of tax-exempt bonds could be imposed. The Tax Reform Act of 1986 imposed a $150 million limit on nonprofit organizations, but hospitals were exempt. The limit was removed in 1997.

[10] Nonprofit hospitals can choose to file for a calendar year or a fiscal year, and their fiscal years vary widely. To ensure that the outstanding stock of tax-exempt debt (obtained from the Form 990 information return) did not include the new bonds issued in 2002, the match used the Form 990 information return whose reporting period immediately preceded the date of the bonds issued in 2002, either the 2001 or 2002 return.

[11] GuideStar-NCCS National Nonprofit Research Database, version 2005b, available at http:// nccsdataweb.urban.org.

[12] Investment assets include both financial assets and physical assets held for investment purposes, such as a medical office building that produces rental income.

[13] Moody's Investors Service measures days of cash on hand as 365 times the sum of cash, savings, and investment assets divided by the operating expenses net of depreciation. In effect, it measures how many days of operating expenses could be covered if they had to be

financed from investment assets and working capital. In 2004, the median days of cash on hand for all rated nonprofit hospitals was 146.3; for all hospitals rated below Baa, 50.6; rated Baa, 108; rated A, 166; rated Aa, 235. See Moody's Investors Service, *Moody's Public Finance Healthcare Ratings* (August 2005), p. 23.

[14] If the distribution of hospitals that borrow using tax-exempt debt varies by size across the years, the dollar figures from the 2002 estimates might be particular to those 310 hospitals and might be too low or too high.

[15] Implementing a broader definition of tax arbitrage would not only reduce the tax preference for those nonprofit hospitals with substantial accumulated investment assets, but also it would also impose a differential cost of capital on those hospitals with and without accumulated investment assets.

[16] Assume a $1,000 taxable bond yields 8 percent and a tax-exempt bond yields 6 percent. A hospital that chose not to use that $1,000 tax-exempt bond would decrease the government's tax expenditure by $20 (calculated as the $1,000 bond times the 8 percent taxable bond rate times the 0.25 income tax rate of the bondholder). A hospital that chose to subject its returns to yield restriction could rebate the returns from tax arbitrage or invest in State and Local Government Series bonds (SLUGS). If it chose to rebate its earnings from tax arbitrage and it was investing in taxable debt, it would rebate $20 (calculated as the taxable bond principal of $1,000 times the difference between the 8 percent taxable bond rate and the 6 percent tax-exempt bond rate). If it chose to buy SLUGS, the federal government's borrowing costs would decline by $20 (calculated as the difference between financing $1,000 of borrowing at 6 percent rather than 8 percent). Of course, hospitals might earn more or less than the taxable bond rate on their investment portfolios, but that only means that the government shares the risk premium on equity investments when a hospital chooses the rebate option.

[17] The estimates are restricted to hospitals that issued tax-exempt debt in 2002. The historical measure could overstate the severity of tax arbitrage for all hospitals if many hospitals issue little or no debt. The historical measure of tax arbitrage for the entire population of hospitals in 2002 (presented in Appendix A) is only slightly smaller (57.8 percent).

[18] No absolute standard exists for what a reasonable allowance of precautionary savings might be. One comparison would be the 135 days' average cash on hand maintained by for-profit hospitals in 2003. That estimate derives from information on 120 such hospitals in California, obtained from combining cost data reported to Medicare and audited financial data from the California Office of Statewide Health Planning and Development.

[19] See William M. Gentry, "Debt Investment and Endowment Accumulation: The Case of Not-forProfit Hospitals," *Journal of Health Economics*, vol. 21, no. 5 (2002), pp. 845-872.

[20] Including state tax preferences would further reduce the nonprofit hospital's cost of capital.

[21] Congressional Budget Office, *The Budget and Economic Outlook: Fiscal Years 2007 to 2016* (January 2006).

[22] The historical real return on equity is estimated by Jeremy Siegel, *Stocks for the Long Run* (New York: McGraw-Hill, 1998).

CHAPTER SOURCES

The following chapters have been previously published:

Chapter 1 – This is an edited, excerpted and augmented edition of a United States Congressional Research Service publication, Report Order Code RL34605, dated May 12, 2010.

Chapter 2 – This is an edited, excerpted and augmented edition of a United States Government Accountability Office publication, Report Order Code GAO-08-880, dated September 2008.

Chapter 3 – This is an edited, excerpted and augmented edition of a United States Congressional Budget Office publication, dated December 2006.

Chapter 4 – This is an edited, excerpted and augmented edition of a United States Congressional Budget Office publication, dated December 6, 2006.

INDEX

D

E

F

G

H

R

S

T